SIX RUSSIAN MEN – LIVES IN TURMOIL

what gives each of
these men meaning
to their lives?

SIX RUSSIAN MEN: LIVES IN TURMOIL

By

EUGENIA HANFMANN

and

HELEN BEIER

THE CHRISTOPHER PUBLISHING HOUSE
NORTH QUINCY, MASS.
02171

PRINTED IN

THE UNITED STATES OF AMERICA

To our Russian respondents.

PREFACE

Of the six Russians whose psychological portraits appear in this book, all but one were born after the October Revolution of 1917 and grew up in the Soviet Union. The vicissitudes of the Second World War and its aftermath brought them to Western Europe; they chose not to return and thus became Displaced Persons.

These six men were among the fifty Soviet Russians whom the authors studied intensively, as part of the Harvard Project on the Soviet Social System conducted by an interdisciplinary team; the data was collected in West Germany in 1950-51. In the following years the main findings of the clinical study of this group were published in journal articles (1,4,5,6,7,9). We had intended from the start to complement group data by a collection of individual case studies, but various other projects took precedence over this one. Although a few case histories have appeared separately (2,3,8), the present book has been greatly delayed.

Had these case studies been published twenty years ago, their main function would have been to depict life as it was lived under Stalin's reign. After the war the Iron Curtain was no longer intact, but the cracks were of recent origin; the abundant eyewitness testimony on the workings of the Soviet system, obtained from former Soviet citizens displaced by the war, was being studied by experts and only gradually reaching the general public. The life histories of our respondents are dramatic illustrations of human fates in Soviet Russia. Regardless of the author's intentions in preparing these case studies, they would have been read at the time for their general, or sociological, interest; their publication would have served to fulfill our subjects' wish "to tell the West". Today the situation is different. The West has been told long ago, and the Soviet regime is not what it was then, though it has not changed

enough to make use of the most potent means of progress, a
frank facing of one's past. These life histories could not be
published in the Soviet Union even today; the information they
contain about the recent past is by no means common knowledge in the country in which these lives had been lived. The
young people in particular are ignorant of the dreadful facts of
Stalin's reign, a period they have not experienced. Some Russian
writers and scientists are currently struggling for the right to
"tell all", convinced that only full candid reports can prevent a
return to the most nightmarish period of Soviet history (14).
But to the West the conditions of life under Stalin are no longer
news, at least not to those who care to know, particularly since
the publication of Solzhenitsyn's works. Not being political
news, the human fates described in this book can now be used
to stimulate our psychological thinking and perhaps enrich us
with new insights. We studied our Russian respondents primarily
as psychologists in the tradition of Harry Murray and Robert
White, interested in tracing the total course of an individual life,
but these cases may be of some value to all students of personality. They touch upon many issues of interest to systematic
psychology.

The most obvious issue lies in the area of *"culture and personality"*: the cases can be used to exemplify the personality
patterns encountered in the Russian group we had studied, the
kind of people our subjects were. Those members of the
Harvard team who were gathering information about the workings of the Soviet social system from large numbers of respondents were instructed to refer for clinical study mainly those who
struck them as "typical Soviet people" sharing the traits of the
majority; they were also asked to include some who were particularly communicative and productive. From the many interesting and appealing people found among the 50 subjects of
the clinical study, we selected these six men as particularly informative, clear-cut, and colorful cases. They also represent, in
stronger relief, the personality patterns we found in the group,
and in approximately the same distribution; four out of six
demonstrate the *"modal pattern"* which was present in about
60 percent of our subjects. A generalized description of the
modal pattern and a discussion of whether it can be equated

with the Russian "national character" will be found in the article by one of us which is reprinted, in part, at the end of this book (5, see also 7).

The subjects of our study have more in common than the same national culture. The *historical and social setting* of their lives has given a similar stamp to their fates. In the lives of our six subjects *catastrophes* have loomed large; though only one had been in a labor camp, all have known extreme deprivation, disruption, and threat. For most of them the blows began to fall early, because of their connection with the peasantry, the social class that as late as 1928 still comprised *ca* 80 percent of the Soviet Union's population. Although not one of our subjects remained a peasant, all of them came from a peasant or quasi-peasant background. The families of most of them were hard hit by the catastrophic events which went with the forced collectivization of agriculture. These events took place in the late twenties and early thirties when our five younger subjects were from five to fifteen years old. For most of them this early disruption was followed by a period of relative security during which these gifted and capable people worked out some adaptation to the new conditions of life. They did this by different means, but not one of them chose to adapt to the totalitarian state by serving the secret police. Our one older subject rose to high rank in the professional army; two were on the way to joining the Soviet elite, one of them was a convinced communist; two became skilled workers making a better than average living; only one remained trapped in abject poverty. But for all of them there was in store another series of catastrophes, which was unleashed by World War II and resulted in their uprooting and permanent displacement from their country. When we studied these men, their present was precarious and their future uncertain.

Life histories that abound in traumatic events lend themselves to the study of the roots and effects of *psychological health and maladjustment,* of conduct reflecting a realistically balanced or a distorted outlook on life. In the study we made of our respondents' level of adjustment (6), two of our six subjects were rated as well adjusted, more balanced than the majority of the clinically studied group, three as average in adjustment, and one as maladjusted, though not as extremely as some. But whatever the ratings, we may expect to find both health and disturbance potentially present in all our subjects, as they are in all people. Adopting the concepts of Andras Angyal (10,11), we may view "health" and "neurosis" as two incompatible outlooks on life which organize the totality of the person's experiences and strivings within two different frameworks— that of hope, of confidence in oneself and others, and that of doubt and diffidence. According to Angyal, there are both healthy and traumatic features in every child's life; the child's early attempts to relate himself to the world succeed in part and in part fail. As a result, personality develops simultaneously around two nuclei and forms two patterns, one or the other of which may be underdeveloped but is never absent. Confidence and diffidence, conviction and doubt that life is livable, mark the "great divide", the point at which the human life course acquires its basic existential conflict and its dual organization. Health and neurosis are not segments of personality; they are total organizations—two dynamic Gestalts organizing the same material, each according to its own system principle, and competing for dominance. The person is neurotic or healthy depending on which system is dominant.

The lives of our subjects, repeatedly shattered by catastrophes, can hardly be described as "lives in progress", a title chosen by R. W. White for his studies of normal young people (15). Yet, in spite of the obstacles to external progress, often impenetrable, the "progressive" trend inherent in these Russians' strivings was no less impressive than it was in the calmer lives of White's subjects: here was self-actualization in adverse circumstances, under conditions producing many internal contradictions and conflicts. In trying to organize some seemingly inconsistent data into coherent personality pictures, we found Angyal's concept of the dual organization of personality, of "universal ambiguity", very illuminating; we used it as a guideline. In turn, the cases serve to elaborate further this theoretical conception by making more concrete and explicit the various manifestations of the two basic patterns postulated by Angyal and the various specific ways in which the dual organization can function. Perhaps one reason why these cases are so informative and attractive is that in most of them both patterns are clear and strong; neither the confident nor the diffident orientation is obscured from view by what Angyal calls the "surface" personality, a front reflecting compliance with conventions. Consequently, whenever dominance shifts from one pattern to the other, the reversals are clearly seen. The life histories of our subjects provide material for conjectures about the preconditions for the "easy reversibility" of the two patterns. They also contain material for studying the factors that further the development of sound personal assets and for elucidating the effects of traumatic experiences occurring at different age levels. Of the more specific issues, the role of *ideological concerns* in personal adjustment is brought into focus by pressures exercised by the totalitarian system. The various personal functions that ideologies can serve (12)—such as orientation, personal expression, internal and external adjustment—are partly modified, partly brought into relief by the regime's policy of denying its citizens the right to varied opinions on political and social issues. Still, opinions do vary and do change under the impact of experience. Our group includes a devoted young communist who later turned anti-Soviet and an atheist who turned Christian as a result of a conversion experience. Whenever our subjects' political and religious beliefs, changed or persisting, threw some light on their personalities (or on the dynamics of beliefs), a discussion of their ideologies was incorporated in the personality studies.

Here are a few words about the methods used in the study. Our main sources of data were extended clinical interviews, informal conversations, and projective tests, all of which we administered and recorded in Russian. We also had at our disposal records of the standard interviews on their lives in Soviet Russia and on their political views that were administered to all respondents of the Harvard Project. We started our own interviewing by asking our subjects to tell us about their lives in exile, their recent and current problems and plans. Later on we explored their earlier life histories, keeping in mind the topics we wanted to cover, but not preventing the respondents from introducing their own topics. Between the two main parts of the interview we presented our subjects with some projective techniques de-

vised to stimulate the person's fantasy and to facilitate an un-
guarded expression of personal feelings and attitudes. We asked
our subjects to interpret meaningless ink blots of the Rorschach
Test; to make stories about the pictures of Murray's Thematic
Apperception Test (TAT) which depicts not too clearly defined
human situations; to answer the Projective Questions that have
been used in the California studies of authoritarianism (16);
to tell, for example, what people they admire, what actions
they abhor, what makes them ashamed or sad. To these standard methods widely used in clinical personality studies we added
three others specifically designed by us for the purposes of our
study: "special TAT" pictures representing recognizable Soviet
situations, such as peasants' meeting, a workshop, a store; one
hundred sentence fragments to be completed; and the "Episodes"
Test, requiring a discussion of problematic interpersonal situations (reproduced in Appendix A). The length of the clinical
study varied for different respondents between two and four
days. More detail about the conduct of the study will emerge
from the case studies themselves; some will be given in the concluding chapter which summarizes the results of the projective
tests obtained from all 50 clinically studied Russian subjects and
an American comparison group.

The case studies themselves are preceded by a chapter out-
lining the periods and events in the history of Soviet Russia
that were of vital importance in the lives of our subjects, both
in their childhood and adulthood. About the presentation of
the cases a few words will suffice. The foci of interest discussed
above—life under stress, deformation and health—have not been
developed into a systematic guide for case analysis nor used as an
outline for case presentation. Each case has been written up so
as to highlight the individual pattern that emerged from the
careful analysis of all data. The data is cited only illustratively,
so as not to burden the presentation with technical detail. We
have tried to make our subjects come alive as individual people
and to share with the reader some of our own vivid experiences
in getting to know them and to appreciate our common humanity. To quote from an earlier publication, "The picture of the
totalitarian methods of control and 'persuasion' that emerged
cumulatively from the life histories of our subjects was frighten-

ingly similar to the psychotic scene depicted by Orwell in *1984*. Yet in spite of the severity of these pressures for inner conformity, and of the crushing blows they had suffered, the majority of the people we studied have in no way become automatons of the kind visualized by Orwell, with the fantastic illogic of the regime substituted for their inner experience. With all their disturbances and twists, fearful anticipations and habits of external obedience and of evasion, many of them showed a genuineness and spontaneity that surprised and delighted the listener" (2, p. 667). We were glad of the chance to know the six people who figure in this book; we are grateful to them for having given us this chance.

CONTENTS

SOVIET HISTORY IN OUTLINE*

The main function of this outline is to provide a background for the case histories by describing those situations and events which had an impact on the lives of our six subjects, as children or adults; it is, therefore, highly selective. Thus, since all our respondents were Russians, we do not touch upon the treatment of national minorities; since our group included no teachers, writers or artists, we bypass cultural policies except the treatment of the church. Apart from wars, foreign and civil, the most powerful pressures on the largest number of Soviet citizens came from the economics policies that shaped their living conditions and from the terror by means of which the totalitarian regime was established and maintained.

We have sketched in the historical background of the Russian revolution and the five periods into which Russian history between 1914 and 1950 (the time of our study) most naturally falls: the breakdown of the old regime and the Bolshevik seizure of power, the Civil War, NEP (New Economic Policy), the rise of totalitarianism, and the Second World War and its aftermath. Of our six subjects, only the oldest one was born years before the revolution, the rest grew up under the Soviet regime.

The Background of the Revolution

The first Slavic state on Russian soil arose in the ninth century in the region of Kiev; in the tenth century Christianity was imported from Byzantium; a period of cultural flowering followed. Soon, however, the Kievan state disintegrated into small independent principalities, with much fighting between their princes. In the thirteenth century the Kievan territory was overrun and conquered by the Mongols who remained in control for over two centuries. This period of subjugation was a setback for the

---

*Based mainly on D. W. Treadgold, *Twentieth Century Russia.* (Chicago: Rand McNally, 1959), and G. Von Rauch, *A History of Soviet Russia.* (New York: Praeger, 1957).

17

country and isolated it from Western influences. The princes of
Moscow — who later came to call themselves Tsars — threw off
the Mongol yoke and began to expand their territory and to
develop a centralized state under a strong autocratic government.
They subjugated the northern trading city-states, dispersed the
popular assemblies which were a restraint on the princes, and,
after crushing the "boyars", the old independent aristocracy,
established a new noble serving class. In return for their support
and their service, the state allowed the gentry to reduce to serfdom the peasants who lived on their newly-granted lands. Peter
the Great, who around 1700 inaugurated a cultural revolution
and opened a "window to Europe", completed the process of
dividing the population into fixed social estates. The old institu-
tion of peasant self-government, the village commune, was now
used to enforce the peasants' fiscal and other obligations to the
state and the landlords. By the end of the eighteenth century
the gentry's obligations to serve the state (as functionaries and
military officers) were abolished and their power over their
serfs became virtually that of private slave owners. However,
they remained excluded from political power. The unlimited
authority of the Tsar was implemented by a bureaucracy whose
powers reached far down into local affairs.

In practice most monarchs were restrained from the extremes
of arbitrariness by the opinions of their advisers, some of whom
were responsible for important reforms, and by their judgment
of the state of mind of the various social classes. As education
spread the political attitudes underwent changes; first the gentry, then the middle classes experienced the impact of the
eighteenth-century enlightenment and of later ideological developments originating in Western Europe. In the course of the
nineteenth century this impact brought forth the phenomenon
of "Russian intelligentsia" — a segment of the educated class
greatly concerned with the state of society in Russia and the
world which became increasingly more radical in its political
goals. The "populists" placed their hope in the peasant commune
as the nucleus of the future socialist order and moved into the
country disticts to preach their gospel in the villages, without
much success. The Tsar's government fought all such subver-
sive activities; radical writers, particularly journalists, were

plagued by the ubiquitous censorship. But unlike Soviet total-itarianism, the old regime never exacted conformity to a set of ideological principles prescribed by the government; this left writers a great deal of freedom. The "Golden Age" of literature in Russia, marked by such names as Pushkin, Gogol, Tolstoy, Turgenev, Dostoevsky, lasted through most of the nineteenth century, both under the oppressive regime of Nicholas I and the milder reign of Alexander II; the first decades of the twentieth century were marked by vigorous new developments both in literature and in the arts.

The old pattern of social organization was greatly modified under Alexander II who in 1861 abolished serfdom. Other reforms gave the freed peasant a share in a new system of self-government and vastly improved the administration of justice, eliminating the old principle of class preferment. Many members of the intelligentsia went to work in the reformed institutions, acquiring experience in democratic processes on a local level. Russia seemed finally to be starting on the path of democratization; the Tsar was actually considering some measures that would limit his autocracy. However, as so often in history, what had been done proved too little and too late. A militant revolutionary movement had developed and was by then locked in a deadly struggle with the government; each blow produced a counterblow. In 1881 a terrorist organization, after having killed many high officials, succeeded in assassinating Alexander II. There have been few more grotesque tragedies than that of the execution or imprisonment of the deeply moral and humanitarian young people who had in their zeal murdered the ruler who had done more to improve the lot of the Russian people than any other monarch in their history.

The next reign, that of Alexander III, was marked by reactionary policies and a lull in the opposition's activities, but the period of calm did not last very long. In the nineties the Party of Socialist Revolutionaries was founded, which could be viewed as heir of the populists; its program centered on agrarian revolution. The PSR had a "Fighting Organization"; this group of would-be political assassins went into action at the beginning of the century. In the wake of the disorders of 1905, while the government was court-martialling revolution-

aries, the terrorists murdered more than 4000 officials and
carried out many robberies to replenish party coffers.   But
while the government considered the terrorists its main enemies,
the future was in the hands of the group guided by a new doctrine—Marxism. A Marxist party, the Russian Social-Democratic
Labor Party, was formed in 1898 and soon split into factions.
The "Bolsheviks" (meaning the majority) headed by Lenin differed from the "Mensheviks" (the minority) in their interpretation of some of the Marxist postulates and in their strategies.
Lenin rejected any collaboration with the despised "bourgeois
liberals"; he insisted that the Party, the elite guardian of Marxist
insights, should be led and controlled by a small tight group of
professional revolutionaries; democracy would come after the
revolution, when the masses had understood these truths. Trotsky (who changed to the Bolshevik faction only in 1917) correctly foresaw at this early time that Leninism would lead to a
situation wherein the organization of the Party takes the place
of the Party itself; the Central Committee takes the place of the
organization; and finally the dictator takes the place of the
Central Committee.
  The existence of militant revolutionary parties engaged in
agitation and prepared to use as tinder whatever discontent
there was, was crucial in the preparation of the revolutions of
1905 and 1917 and in their later fate. The disorders of 1905
were precipitated by military defeats in the war with Japan and
the ensuing disorganization; they fed on the peasants' discontent
with too little land and too many burdens, a discontent which
through the centuries had erupted in occasional revolts, and on
the grievances of industrial workers whose pay was low and
whose conditions of life were miserable. There was a genuine
mass involvement of workers and peasants, a wave of general
strikes and uprisings, but the participants were far from unani-
mous in their goals. All revolutionary parties sought to provide
them with leaders and with slogans for the expression of their
grievances. The newly-formed Councils (Soviets) of Workers'
Deputies were used to rally the urban workers to the support
of radical political programs, diverting them from the struggle
for immediate economic betterment within the existing order.
The revolution of 1905 wrested several important reforms

from the Tsar. His October Manifesto granted civil liberties—which were later abridged—and a legislative assembly, the State Duma. The Duma was elected by the population and controlled much of the budget, but its powers were far short of those of the British House of Commons. The ministers remained appointive; the Tsar's successive choices reflected his vacillation between different influences.

The constitutional reform did not heal the rift between the government and liberal public opinion, despite the efforts of the prime minister, Stolypin, the most capable official of the last Tsar's reign. Some of the revolutionary parties at first boycotted elections to the Duma; later their delegates tried to disrupt it from inside; they shared with the rightists the goal of preventing the Duma from functioning. Eventually they were excluded, and suffrage was drastically curtailed. Stolypin, a constitutional monarchist, pursued the double goal of order and reform. He countered the Socialist Revolutionaries' renewed terror by widespread arrests; within a few years the chief leaders of the revolutionary parties were driven abroad or exiled to Siberia. In working together with the more moderate Third Duma, despite opposition from the Right and the Left, Stolypin helped to enact progressive laws, e.g., the law decreeing gradual establishment of compulsory education. His chief enterprise was the attempt to solve the agrarian problem by helping those peasants who wished to do so to abandon the village commune and become individual Western-style farmers, working a single contiguous plot of land; this could be cultivated more effectively than the scattered strips of land formerly allotted for their use by the traditional policy in an attempt to secure a fair distribution of better and poorer plots. This plan met with strong response from the land-hungry peasants even though the reshuffling of holdings required extremely complex surveying operations. By 1917 two-thirds of the peasant households had initiated the proceedings, while one-tenth had completed them and had become independent farmers. The lands left to the landlords at Emancipation were gradually passing from their increasingly inefficient hands to the peasants, who seemed to be closer than they had ever been to realizing their old dream of tilling their own land.

Under Stolypin's ministry the Tsarist government made its last best effort; when he was murdered (by a double agent) the government passed into much less competent hands and was often influenced by the personal affairs of the court; the "holy man" Rasputin owed his influence to the Empress's belief in his power to preserve the life of the hemophilic heir who stood in danger of dying from any slight injury.

The Breakdown of the Old Regime and the
Bolshevik Seizure of Power: 1914–1918

In the European crisis of 1914 the Russian government, which traditionally tended to protect the small Slav countries, supported Serbia against Austria's military threat by declaring general mobilization; this was one of the acts that unleashed World War I. Russia was poorly prepared for war on a large scale and in no condition to rally quickly. The difficulty was not caused by any lack of basic resources. Though still largely an agricultural country, Russia had started on the path of industrialization soon after the emancipation of the serfs in 1861, had made striking progress during the nineties and, by 1913, had become one of the major producer nations. Education was moving in the direction of mass instruction; the sale of books, the number of schools of all levels were on the increase, and the literacy level was impressively high both in the cities and in the country (it later sank sharply during the years of war, revolution and civil war). The population offered no resistance to the war; there was, in fact, an initial spurt of patriotic feeling which served to create harmony and to make the Tsar once more the national symbol. The Duma voted war credits and even some of the Socialists gave limited support to the war effort. But the government was in the hands of grossly incompetent ministers. They failed to take advantage of the public support in organizing the country's material and human resources. The railway network was not adequately maintained, no effective measures were taken to buttress the economy against the strains of war, and the recruits lacked proper training and equipment.

The war brought some successful offensives, some disastrous defeats, and staggering casualties; the reverses caused a growing public alarm. The progressive parties of the Duma demanded

that the government institute various reforms to increase national unity and appoint to positions of leadership persons
whom the country trusted. These demands were not met—the
new appointments reflected Rasputin's influence. In December
of 1916 Rasputin was assassinated by a group of courtiers and
conservatives; the country was full of rumors of coming change.
In February, crowds rioted in Petrograd (now Leningrad) against
the shortage of bread in the capital, and the troops called to
control them soon changed to their side. The discredited regime
offered no resistance to the revolt which overnight turned into
revolution. A provisional government was formed by the major
parties of the Left and Center; simultaneously, a group of men
formed the Petrograd Soviet of Workers' Deputies, modelled
on the institutions prominent in the events of 1905. Within a
few days most of the old cabinet was under arrest, Nicholas
abdicated in favor of his brother, who prudently refused, and
the "bloodless revolution" was victorious. The monarchy's fall
was quick and complete.

The February Revolution proclaimed the advent of democratic principles. The Provisional Government enacted legislation granting civil liberties to all and announced as its main objective a Constituent Assembly, which generations of revolutionaries had clamored for. The Assembly, to be elected by universal suffrage, was to decide on Russia's new form of government and on the most pressing economic and social reforms.
There was general rejoicing over the newly gained freedom and
hopes for a better future for all.

In later years there was to be much soul-searching and much
mutual recrimination among the non-communist Russian intelligentsia about who had lost the February Revolution, thus enabling the Bolsheviks to take over. Some believe that Russia's
chance for a democratic development was forfeited by the
Provisional Government which insisted that all major decisions,
including the conditions of peace, must await the Constituent
Assembly, yet failed to convene it immediately. The government's power to deal with pressing issues was also undermined
by the presence of an influential rival agency, the Soviets, and
by the socialists' uncertainty about the role they were to play
at that stage. Kerensky, a socialist, was a member of the Provi-

sional Government from the start; but most Marxists felt that
the workers' party would compromise itself if it were to assume
political power prematurely: since Russia was a backward country, only just entering the stage of "bourgeois revolution", it
was unripe for socialism. Consequently, the socialists, while
wielding wide influence, gave little support to the government,
though they actually shared most of its goals. The Bolshevik
position was different. Lenin was adept at fitting the doctrine
to the demands of the moment, and he was in command of an
organization resembling a military unit more than a political
party. He saw and seized the opportunity of conquering power
over the heads of the other parties, including the socialists. The
latters' unwillingness to go against the "laws of history" opened
a gap in the ranks of the supporters of the February Revolution;
the Bolsheviks, after skillfully maneuvering themselves into the
control of the Soviet, were able to drive through this gap with
an ease which surprised even themselves. Shortly before the
Constituent Assembly was to meet Lenin staged an armed uprising, the October Revolution; the coup was carried out in
Petrograd with the help of pro-Bolshevik troops; following this,
local Bolshevik detachments of workers and soldiers seized
power in most other cities in Russia. At first Lenin still pretended to sponsor the Constituent Assembly, but actually the
Bolsheviks (who later changed their name to Communists) were
on the way to one-party dictatorship. When the elections gave
60 percent of the seats to the Socialist Revolutionaries and
only 25 percent to the Bolsheviks, the Constituent Assembly
was dispersed without much ado after meeting just once. Soon
most of the political parties were outlawed, the old organs of
self-government dissolved, and Red Terror launched by the
Cheka, the first variant of the secret police.

The new government of Soviets, never more than a front for
the Party, negotiated a separate peace with Germany. Private
property was abolished and all private and church lands were
transferred to the Soviets of Peasant Deputies for distribution
to peasants. This decree legalized what the peasants had, in fact,
already done. Once the discipline in the army had collapsed, the
peasant-soldiers had deserted en masse and gone home to carry
out an agrarian revolution of their own, seizing the landlords'

remaining estates. The Soviet government did not interfere with the resulting distribution of land until a decade later.

Civil War and War Communism: 1918—1921

The armed struggle against the Bolshevik regime was organized by leaders of other political parties who had participated in the Provisional Government, by former officers, and by members of national minorities who sought independence, with Ukrainians in the vanguard. It was not a centrally organized effort; different groups and military leaders came up one after another, and their policies differed. In some of its stages the White movement was supported by a rather halfhearted Allied intervention and by the so-called Czechoslovak Legion, which had fought in the World War on the Russian side; newly independent Poland launched an offensive in support of the Ukraine's independence. Bitter fighting raged over wide expanses of Russian territory, including Siberia. The threat to the Soviets was very real, but eventually the Red Army, effectively trained by Trotsky, was victorious in most parts of the old Russian empire; the main exceptions were those border territories which had become independent national states (Finland, Estonia, Latvia, Lithuania, and Poland). But, although the Civil War was at an end, the hoped for revolution in the West had not come, and there was serious trouble inside Russia.

In the organization of the economy, the years of the Civil War were the years of "War Communism". The economic measures of this period were in part an attempt to realize the party's ideological goals, in part an effort to get the needed support for the war. In 1918 the government nationalized all major industries; many of the old managers soon had to be brought back, however, to end the disorganization resulting from "workers' control"; now the workers were subjected to increasingly strict control by the state. At the same time an unsuccessful attempt was made to "carry the class war to the village" by inciting the poorest peasants to fight the richer ones (the "kulaks"). The peasantry refused to "split" and to conduct its own civil war. The village "Committees of the Poor" were supposed to requisition the grain needed to feed the cities, but actually the requisitioning was done by Communists from the cities. Private trade was prohibited.

These measures imposed additional hardships on people who had suffered disruption and impoverishment during the years of fighting; their discouragement turned into hostility. At the end of the Civil War there were peasant uprisings in different places and a wave of strikes in Petrograd; these strikes were supported by sailors, mostly peasant recruits, and culminated in the Kronstadt uprising which proclaimed the slogan, "Soviets without Communists". Red forces shot down thousands and quelled the revolt.

Lenin's New Economic Policy;
Stalin's Rise to Power: 1921—1928

Faced with the breakdown of the economy and widespread discontent among the peasants, Lenin temporarily retreated from Communist objectives. The new economic policy (NEP) replaced the requisitioning of agricultural surpluses with tax in kind; the peasant had to deliver 10 percent of his produce to the government but could sell the remainder on the free market. Peasants were now also permitted to lease land and hire labor. Heavy industry remained a governmental enterprise, but the small businessman was granted a measure of economic freedom. This mixed system, which left some space for private enterprise, quickly resulted in a revival of the economy and stabilization of the regime. By 1928 the indices of production were generally back to what they had been in 1914. Many peasants expected NEP to be permanent, and many foreign observers decided—not for the last time—that the Soviet leaders were abandoning all Communist aspirations. NEP turned out to be only a breathing space, a partial respite from state interference. Ordinary Soviet citizens, including most of those interviewed by the Harvard Project soon after the war, remember this period as the least harsh, the most normal one in Soviet history. During these years a struggle was raging at the top levels of the Party over which leader and which policy would determine the fate of the people, but the people themselves were mostly left alone to lead their own lives.

In 1924 Lenin died, and his death was an important landmark in Stalin's rise to power. There had never been much democracy in the organization of the Party, the authority having been vested in the Politburo (Political Bureau of the Central Committee of the Party), the actual governing body of the country. As time went on divergent opinions were tolerated less and less. Already under Lenin all factions within the Party were outlawed; following this a nationwide purge was carried out and almost one-third of the Party members were expelled. At that time, a reformed secret police was given the right to arrest Party members. Stalin, one of the old-timers in the Party, was careful never to contradict Lenin, and he steadily acquired more influence; by the time of Lenin's illness he was entrenched in a number of important government and Party posts. Lenin, in his political testament, pointed out that Stalin had concentrated enormous power in his hands and was unlikely to use it with sufficient caution; he was preparing an open attack on Stalin at the next Party Congress, but suffered a stroke before he could carry it out.

In the course of the next few years, Stalin defeated his rivals, including Trotsky, and, through adroit use of the Party apparatus, brought under his control the secret police and the army. As always, the struggle for personal power among the Communist leaders was at the same time a debate on the best and fastest way to realize the Communist program at home and abroad. Viewed schematically, the "Left" advocated a rapid passage from the bourgeois to the socialist state and hoped for a revolution in the West; the "Right" was in favor of continuing NEP, which assured the peasants' support, and a slow transition to socialism. Stalin's position was different in different stages, but eventually he contributed the thesis of "socialism in one country"; the Party could and should build socialism in Russia, without waiting for world revolution; the country's tremendous natural resources would enable the Russian workers to accomplish the task on their own. Stalin's opponents recanted or were exiled: he was hailed as "the Lenin of today". The way had been prepared for one-man rule.

"The Great Change" and the Consolidation
of Totalitarianism: 1928–1941

"The Great Change" (called by some the Second Revolution) began with the First Five-Year Plan (1928–1932) in both in-

dustry and agriculture. Having silenced all dissidents, particularly those who advocated more gradual changes by persuasion
rather than force, Stalin decided to industrialize rapidly, and to
industrialize the countryside as well as the city. By then the
peasantry, i.e., the great majority of the population, consisted
almost entirely of smallholders, who in working their land used
largely their own and their families' labor. These millions of
people who had tenaciously held on to their land were to be
converted into a landless agricultural proletariat, so that the
Communist ideals might be realized; the change was also to solve
the government's current problems.

It was hoped, in accordance with Marxist beliefs, that once
the economy was put into a socialist mold, and the entire labor
force, rural as well as urban, had become employees of state-
controlled enterprises, the "superstructure" of attitudes arising
on the economic "foundation" would also change. No longer
would the regime be troubled by the attachment of the peasantry to its land, the ambivalence of workers about their "real"
interests, the persistence of religious beliefs and prerevolutionary values in the family; the masses' indifference or hostility to
the aims of the materialist and socialist Soviet state would become a thing of the past. The human factor was largely left out
of the oversimplified ideological equation, but still resistance
was expected, even if it may have been underestimated: the saying that one cannot make an omelette without breaking eggs
was widely quoted among the leaders. The total program was
to be carried out by employing all the power of the state to
strengthen control over all branches of economic, social, and
cultural life. Nominally, the First Five-Year Plan was an economic scheme only; in actual fact it inaugurated a new phase in
Russian history, in which governmental fiat invaded every area
of life in a manner unparalleled not only in Russia but in any
other country up to that time. The Plan marked the real beginning of Soviet totalitarianism.

Collectivization of agriculture and "liquidation of kulaks as
a class" were carried out in an extremely brutal way, indeed
laden with sheer horror. The wealthier peasants and anyone
who resisted inclusion in collective farms were deported, families separated; military detachments attacked resisting villages;

bloodshed and chaos reigned in the countryside. Large numbers resorted to passive resistance by killing their livestock and burning their crops. The destruction of the peasant households and the ravage of the countryside resulted in a severe famine; this man-made famine was never acknowledged by the Soviet government; not many in the rest of the world were aware of the catastrophe. By a conservative estimate, at least five million peasants died as a result of collectivization including those who died of starvation. The long-term economic damage was also disastrous; the number of horses and cattle at the end of the First Plan was less than half of the 1928 figure; the pre-1928 per capita level of all agricultural production was not regained until years later.

By 1937, 90 percent of peasant families were reported collectivized but their resistance had not been entirely in vain: it had forced the communists to permit each household to retain his own tiny garden plot and its livestock. In all future years these garden plots accounted for a disproportionately high percentage of the total agricultural produce. Forced work in kolkhozes (collective farms) strictly controlled by the state did not turn peasants socialist; their rejection of collectivization was shared by other classes. All Russian informants questioned by the Harvard Project accepted state ownership of large industry, but almost without exception they advocated returning the land to the peasants. However, even if attitudes remained unchanged, the political victory was the state's. The struggle on the agricultural "front" continued, but the victory of the Party over the peasantry was decisive enough so that a battle of such dimensions need not be fought again. The collectivization of agriculture enabled the regime to obtain from the defeated villages much of the capital needed for industrialization — largely by selling at high prices the compulsory grain deliveries, received at a nominal valuation. The political consequences were still greater. Collectivization was the decisive step in the building of the Soviet totalitarian police state: it imposed on the majority of the people a subjection which only force could maintain.

Industrialization achieved spectacular results during the First Five Year Plan (which was declared fulfilled at the end of the 4th year); it continued in subsequent years with unremitting pressure and haste. To provide a stable labor force, millions of peasants were conscripted into industry by agreements made between industrial managers and kolkhoz chairmen; legislation provided that the worker must go wherever he was sent by authorities. To raise productivity, competition between workers was introduced as well as wage differentials and payment of piece work. Staggering records of output achieved by individual workers ("Stakhanovites") were highly rewarded with pay and honors, and their records were used to raise the general norm. Insistence on overfulfilling the quota led to shoddy work and many spurious or fraudulent achievement records. In the late thirties the most stringent compulsion was applied to the labor force: "absenteeism", which included arriving 20 minutes late to work, was penalized by compulsory work in the same enterprise at three-quarters of the usual wages. The trade unions, which in the preceding years (particularly under NEP) had had some weight in industrial enterprizes, were converted into organs of state control over the workers and no longer gave them protection. Collective agreements between trade unions and management were abolished, strikes prohibited, wages and hours fixed by law or the central planning machinery. The unions' functions were reduced to conducting propaganda among the workers and deciding which workers were to go to which sanatoriums for short rests.

The prospect of "building socialism" through industrialization may have fired the enthusiasm of communist believers, but for the majority of people life was hectic and harsh. Consumers' goods were scarce, and promises were continuously made by the leaders of better days to come. The population was controlled not only by propaganda but also by increased terror. With the First Plan inaugurated, the secret police started arresting not only "kulaks" but also the private entrepreneurs, "Nepmen", mainly to lay hands on the wealth they had accumulated. During the years of this plan, one group of engineers were accused of "wrecking" for Germany, another of working for France, a group of "planners" was said to have acted for the émigrés; all charges were known to be false. Stalin obviously used the device of widely publicized "show trials" to frighten the specialists trained in prerevolutionary days into doing what he now demanded of them and to silence all the critics.

Then the terror grew and spread. Although the opposition within the Party had been effectively silenced earlier, in the middle thirties arrests of alleged supporters of the Right and the Left resumed. Then came the turn of the Party elite. The purge culminated in the bloodbath of the "year of damnation", 1937. The trial of sixteen old Bolsheviks was followed by those of lesser-ranking leaders and of army generals, among them the popular Marshal Tukhachevskii. Almost without exception, the accused confessed to the highly implausible crimes imputed to them, such as plotting to overthrow the Communist state and "restore capitalism"; they were speedily executed. The purges widened to include most members of the Party's Central Committee, the highest ranks in the army, most central trade union committees, many managers, intellectuals, Party functionaries and foreign Communists. With this mass of people to process, the continuous interrogation over several days and nights proved too time-consuming; to speed matters up, corporal punishment and torture were legalized in 1938 for the purpose of obtaining confessions. Outside the Party, a multitude of ordinary citizens were also accused; orders went out to the secret police to arrest a certain percentage of the whole population, varying slightly from district to district. Whether Stalin was deranged, as some assume, or was seeking more and more power for himself, or felt that any person not terrorized into complete submission was potentially an enemy, he was certainly successful in securing dictatorial powers. Shaken and weakened by the purges, the basic institutions of the system became more reliable tools of Stalin and the remaining elite. The people at large came to see that there was no safety for them at all; informers were everywhere, with their own quotas to fulfill. By the time the mass purges ended — with the execution of the head of the secret police who had conducted them — an estimated eight million people had been shot or sent to prisons and camps.

The so-called corrective labor camps operated by NKVD (the secret police) soon became the central feature of the Soviet penal system and an important part of the economic setup;

their network covered Northern Russia and Siberia. During the thirties NKVD became the largest single employer in the Soviet Union. It had at its disposal a convict labor force estimated by the most thorough study available at ten million (estimates ranged from two to twenty million). The work in camps was of a very exacting kind (road and canal building, wood cutting); it was performed with the most primitive tools, at wretched levels of remuneration, often in sub-zero temperatures, and in conditions of constant abuse. Failure to fulfill the very high work norm resulted in immediate reduction of food rations, so that the weak and inefficient were weeded out by slow starvation. Those who survived could never be certain that the end of the term to which they had been sentenced would bring freedom: the terms could be arbitrarily extended, even more than once. After their release, the former inmates were limited in their rights and opportunities, as were also the dekulakized peasants and their children. The segment of the population familiar with life in the camps had a notion very different from that of the uninitiated of the real meaning of "personality cult", a term used by the Soviet press in later years to denote and explain Stalin's reign.

The War and the Postwar Period: 1941–1950

The years which witnessed the rise of Soviet totalitarianism were also the years of the Nazis' rise to power. Courted as a likely ally both by Hitler and by the Western powers, the Soviet Union shocked the world by concluding, in August 1939, a trade treaty and a nonaggression pact with Germany. A secret article divided much of Eastern Europe between them, the Soviets getting Finland, Estonia, Latvia, and Bessarabia. Hitler invaded Poland a week later; the Soviet expansion was carried out in stages. The Baltic states were easily induced to sign mutual assistance pacts and were later "admitted" into the Soviet Union as constituent republics, but Finland resisted for several months. The Finnish war and the military occupation of the Baltic states afforded Russian soldiers a glimpse of life outside the Soviet Union, which proved an eye-opener for many.

Before invading Russia (in June 1941) Hitler overran much of Europe, defeated France, and acquired new allies. His plans for an attack on Russia had been made long before he carried them out, but Stalin did not heed the warnings of the British Intelligence and seems to have been surprised by the German attack. The initial thrust of Hitler's armies penetrated deep into the Russian territory; most industrial regions were seized by the Germans; about three million Soviet prisoners were taken during the first six months of fighting. Yet the Germans failed to take Moscow and Leningrad (though during the blockade of the latter over half a million inhabitants starved to death). The demoralizing effect of this failure, the severe Russian winter, the increasingly strong resistance of the Russians, the American lend-lease deliveries, and some errors in Hitler's military strategy all played their part in the reversal of the fortunes of war. The fierce battle of Stalingrad, which lasted months, marked the turning point in 1942, at the time of the Allied victories in North Africa. The Russian armies began moving westward; they crossed the Soviet borders in 1944 and, together with the Allied armies, brought the war in Europe to a close in the spring of 1945.

The first weeks of the war revealed to the Germans—and to many a shocked Soviet leader—that the millions ruled by Stalin hated the regime; having been kept ignorant of the nature of Nazism, they welcomed the invaders as liberators. The peasants in particular expected the Germans to abolish the collective farms and to reopen churches; in many occupied localities they did this themselves. Had the Germans not been committed to the notion of their being a "master race" to be served by the subhuman Slavs, the course of the War in Russia might have been very different. The Germans gave some support to the Ukrainian separatists, but the foundations of the Nazi occupation policy were never altered. This policy soon revealed its full savagery, worse in Russia than anywhere else; hundreds of thousands of prisoners died of hunger and cold in Nazi camps. Their fate was made worse by the attitude of their own government: those taken prisoner were viewed as traitors and given no help through the International Red Cross. Still, Hitler proved no better than Stalin, and the Russians' patriotism was aroused. The partisans, supported by the population, became a grave threat to the Germans, although some of the partisan units were only nominally pro-Soviet and some, like the Ukrainian ones, were openly anti-Soviet.

As popular feeling began to turn against the Nazis, and the strength of the partisans grew, some German army leaders looked for ways to counteract this development. Many tried to persuade Hitler to turn to account the prisoners' wish to fight Stalin's regime. A prominent Soviet general, Andrew Vlasov captured in 1942, was the most suitable candidate for leading an anti-Soviet Russian army; he met with considerable popular response in the occupied territory. But the Germans were not prepared to sponsor the organization of a large-scale Russian "army of liberation", since this would mean sponsoring an independent Russian state in the future. In 1944, close to defeat, Hitler permitted Vlasov to state publicly his anti-Communist democratic position and to form two Russian-Ukrainian free divisions, but by then it was too late to fight the Soviet army. The allied military command viewed Vlasov simply as a traitor to his country; after the war he and his army were turned over to the Soviet authorities. Soon *Pravda* announced the execution of Vlasov and his officers, describing them merely as German agents.

Unlike Hitler, Stalin was very successful in his wartime propaganda, both at home and abroad. In his first war speech he declared that now, as during Napoleon's invasion, Russia was waging a "national patriotic war"; he called for "scorched-earth policy" during retreat and for guerilla warfare in the Nazi-occupied area. The propaganda tactic of nationalism was continued through the war years. Stalin threatened the inhabitants of German-occupied territories with death for treason, i.e., any cooperation with the Germans. But, in his appeals to the people, he also invoked the "manly images of our ancestors", including medieval saints and tsarist generals and, in effect, begged the soldiers to fight for Mother Russia. This pose was his best hope for gaining the support of his subjects, and it also proved most useful to him in relations with the Allies. Seeing him act as the heir of the Tsars, they readily assumed that Soviet interest in world revolution was a thing of the past. Stalin supported this notion by disbanding the Comintern.

The war years provided a breathing space for the Russian writers, a period of relative freedom from censorship and official ideological "guidance". The expression of any emotion was encouraged that could cause the reading public to identify with the struggle against Hitler: patriotism, love, even religion. Earlier Stalin had fought religion head-on; a great number of churches were closed, church bells seized, many of the remaining monasteries dissolved, the Kazan Cathedral in Leningrad was turned into an anti-religious museum; teaching religion was forbidden; a number of high clergy fell during the Great Purges. Still, in spite of the efforts of the League of Militant Godless, the anti-religious campaign fell short of the desired success. The census of 1937 included a question about religious belief. The entire census results were declared faulty and they were not published. One reason for their suppression must have been the population deficiency they recorded, which resulted from collectivization and the early stages of the purges. However, persistent rumors suggested another important reason: 40 percent of the population were said to have declared their religious faith.

During the war, the state resumed relations with the Orthodox Church, permitted the election of a Patriarch, and granted certain facilities for public worship. In return, the Patriarchs proved willing to support the Soviet state policy in domestic and foreign affairs, thus making themselves into the regime's tools; some must have felt that the chance to keep the faith of the people alive by holding religious services was worth any price. The church's cooperation has not been rewarded in any essential way. The League of the Godless was disbanded, but, contrary to reports of some uninformed Western visitors, anti-religious activity has continued; religion, strictly controlled by the state, has made no gains. The changes in official policy at first aroused great hopes. Given the general feeling of national solidarity created by the war, they led people to expect major changes after the war: more freedom, less harshness, some contact with the rest of the world. Stalin deliberately fostered these hopes in his propaganda but had no intention to fulfill them.

The first postwar years witnessed Soviet expansion in Europe, both within and beyond the limits outlined by international agreements. Reports of Soviet ruthlessness, of obstacles placed in the way of Western representatives, of restrictions on freedom in Eastern Europe were rapidly accumulating. In 1946

Winston Churchill spoke of an "iron curtain" having descended across the continent from Stettin on the Baltic to Trieste on the Adriatic. The United States formulated its policy of containment, and the "cold war" was on; under American leadership further Communist expansion in Europe was checked by the end of the forties, while the Soviet satellites were progressing to the stages of collectivization and purges.

Within Russia itself, as a result of the war, living conditions were more miserable than ever: much of the country had been utterly devastated, industry had been wrecked, and half of the railway network destroyed. The Fourth Five-Year Plan initiated in 1946 was to make good all the economic damage.

Those Soviet citizens whom the end of the war found in the West were living through difficult years. Stalin had been remarkably successful in concealing from the West the depth of disaffection which the Soviet people had demonstrated at the beginning of the war, just as he had succeeded in concealing the full extent of terror and destruction that had accompanied collectivization. When the war ended, he wanted to cover the traces of mass hostility to the Soviet regime by speedy repatriation of some three million Soviet citizens still beyond the reach of the Red Army. At the Yalta Conference it was agreed to repatriate all war prisoners, an arrangement that seemed reasonable to the Allies. They cooperated fully with the Soviet repatriation commissions.

For many prisoners of war and other displaced persons the attraction of home prevailed over hostility to the Soviet regime, at least until they found out that the Soviet authorities tended to regard them as criminals and to send them to correctional labor camps rather than home. Others were determined from the start to stay in the West at any cost. Some DPs (displaced persons) escaped repatriation by posing as inhabitants of areas beyond the former Soviet borders, but they were the lucky minority. Men and women killed themselves in large numbers rather than going back. One of the episodes bitterly remembered by the displaced took place in 1945 in Kemten where American troops broke into a church in which the Russians had sought refuge, clubbed them and dragged them out and threw them into trucks for transportation to the Soviet assembly point.

Forcible repatriation was officially halted by the Allies only in 1947; it was still a very recent past for those interviewed by the Harvard Project in 1950, though most of them realized that the Americans' actions had been based on ignorance. The status of those who defected from Soviet control after the war was legalized by the Allies in 1948; before that the West turned deserters back to be shot. But even in 1950 the inmates of DP camps, many of whom were being processed for immigration to the United States or Australia, did not feel safe. Many obstacles were still being put in their way by unreasonable rulings: the United States barred from immigration both former Party or Komsomol members and former Vlasovites. Abductions of prominent former Soviet citizens by the Russian secret police were not infrequent, and persistent rumors were circulated about imminent war between the Soviets and the West. In these circumstances, many DPs felt that acting as respondents for the Harvard Project meant taking great chances; only the mediation of their own organization and guaranteed anonymity made this enterprise possible.

Chapter 1

MICHAEL—A COLONEL IN THE RED ARMY

A. Life History

Michael, fifty-three years old in 1950, had been a high commanding officer in the Red Army until the late thirties, when he was accused of treason and sent to a labor camp. Released into the army during the war, he was soon taken prisoner by the Germans. After the war he managed to escape repatriation; at the time of the study he was being processed for immigration to the United States.

The oldest son of a large family, Michael (hereafter indicated as M) grew up in a village in central Russia. He thought of himself as being of peasant origin: "Ours was a working family, we did not have much land; everyone worked, we had hired help only in summer. I consider myself a peasant. My father even held the position of the village commissar when he died; this was before Party membership was required for it. In the pre-collectivization period I knew the village life well." Actually the father, though he did work the land, belonged to the rural intelligentsia—he was the teacher of the village school. He wanted his children to move upward socially, and M was sent to high school; in accordance with his father's wishes, he planned to become a high school teacher himself, mathematics being his chosen subject. The First World War interfered with these plans. M was drafted before he had a chance to get a university education. He served through the war as an officer and soon after the October Revolution was taken into the Red Army.

M had not previously been in touch with the revolutionary movement, and he had shared the officers' bitterness about the disorganization of the army under the Provisional Government. But he was strongly impressed by Lenin's attack on social inequality and also by his declaration that the soldiers had "voted with their legs" in deserting the front for the home village. He

38

went through a period of re-evaluation of his beliefs, feeling disillusioned about the formerly idealized liberal intelligentsia,
who, he now decided, had loved only the idea of the people,
not the real peasant. He emerged from this period with a willingness to serve the "worker-peasant" regime loyally.

M's conversion to Soviet loyalty and Soviet patriotism makes
excellent sense psychologically, if one considers that his early
identification was divided between the downtrodden peasants
and the intelligentsia, whose superiority he both exaggerated
and resented and whose ranks he was about to join. The disap-
pointing breakdown of the Provisional Government, the government of the intelligentsia, facilitated his rebellion against this
overvalued idol, who, M now saw, did not have the support of
the people. Allegiance to the new leadership provided an excellent solution for the conflict of the double identification. As
an officer of the Red Army, M could enjoy his high status without feeling that he was betraying the group he had left; he was
serving the worker-peasant state and, in the Civil War, he felt he
was fighting the former oppressors.

The change of allegiance was an important event in M's life,
but its psychological significance should not be overestimated:
his emotional attitudes and basic beliefs remained unchanged.
In spite of being disillusioned in the all-too-timid liberalism of
the intelligentsia and resenting their self-glorification, he was
already a member of this group when his change of heart took
place. Their values and frames of reference were an integral
part of himself, and he saw no need to revise them; he believed
that the harshness of the dictatorial revolutionary regime was
only temporary and should subside with complete victory over
its enemies. Thus, the act of giving his loyalty to the new government was not based on a radical conversion; and, in fact, he did
not join the Party. When, a few years later, he was first dis-
criminated against (barred from attending a military academy)
because of not being a Party member, he was deeply shocked.
With the increased pressure for conformity, he felt increasingly
less at ease in his identification with the regime. During the
period of collectivization he had episodic attacks of hatred
toward it for destroying the peasant households and causing
untold suffering. In our interviews M appeared as a typical

prerevolutionary *intelligent,* both in his attitudes and in his style of speech and expression. He drew freely on quotations from Russian classics, was singularly free of Soviet ideological jargon, and did not manifest any specific army spirit or mentality. One could easily imagine him as a prerevolutionary teacher, journalist, or physician who found satisfaction in his work and whose revolutionary sympathies were not sufficiently compelling to make him join the active ranks. Had M been born twenty years earlier he would probably have conformed to this image.

As it was, he could obtain satisfactions from his army career that were sound and strong enough to enable him to repress his uneasiness and his misgivings about the increasingly ugly Soviet reality; he also kept in check his irritation about the disruption and inefficiency caused by the multiple authorities in the army. Having risen to higher rank he was able to exercise leadership and initiative; he enjoyed working with the soldiers, to whom he felt close, who liked and trusted him, and he enjoyed the companionship of his fellow officers; he accepted without compunction the rewards of status, including material advantages, as being earned by ability and hard work. "I liked the absence of routine in my work, the opportunity we had for a wide range of studies, the opportunity for advancement, and the fact that there was no gulf between the officers and the soldiers. I worked hard to prepare myself for leadership and trained my officers in the same way; this gave me great satisfaction." To these satisfactions were added those of family and home; he had married a girl from the prerevolutionary merchant class, had a daughter to whom he was devoted, and enjoyed the relaxation and comfort provided by his well-ordered traditional home run by his wife and her mother.

His own life being basically satisfying to him, M found ways to minimize the disturbing features of Soviet life, from many of which he himself was sheltered. He admitted to us that if he himself had not been arrested and faced with fantastic accusations, he might even have believed in the existence of plots among the military; he had a strong need to believe that there had been some justification for the execution of his hero, Marshal Toukhachevsky, and the chief army generals. The personal experience of arrest was an eye-opener for M, a vivid demonstration of the parody on law and justice staged by the regime. This pretense and deceit, "the net of lies", repelled him more than the idea of open terror. M won the battle with his interrogators that lasted through twelve days of almost uninterrupted questioning; despite threats and inducements, he refused to sign a confession of treason and espionage and to implicate others, even those who had presumably denounced him. This is how he told the story:

> "I told them, what do you want of me? You say you have the evidence against me, so why don't you just go ahead and shoot me. But they wanted me to name others. I told them I wanted to die with a clear conscience. 'Don't argue, scoundrel—sign it!' They insulted me. One of them who knew me well started talking very warmly about my wife and daughter and I was convulsed with crying; he wanted to make use of my feelings for them. They insulted me, but they did not beat me. I thought, if he slaps me, I'll hit him with the chair. . . .I gave them a real battle and I did not sign."

The subsequent years in camps were spent with people from all walks of life herded into camps during the purges; their stories gave M a wide panorama of life as lived under the Soviets. He arrived at the conclusion that the idealism of Lenin and of the other early revolutionaries was dead; means had turned into ends, and the only goal of the Stalin regime was preservation of power at any cost. Yet when released into the army, he fought dutifully and, encircled by the Germans, did not surrender until the ammunition was spent. He would have returned to Russia after the war, even if it were merely "to die in a kolkhoz", if he could have been sure of personal safety.

Now, outside of Russia, M felt unneeded, without any personal future. Although he talked about fighting Stalin and hoped for a war, his anger turned less against the regime that had caused his self-expatriation than against those who at present looked down at him—either as a Russian, or as a Soviet citizen, or as a pitiful person without a country. He ascribed such disparaging views to the Westerners, or to the old émigrés; the latter represented the old intelligentsia he had rejected. M was one of those by no means exceptional respondents who, far from trying to flatter the Americans, displayed increased Soviet patriotism in the face of criticism of their country; he did not for a moment renounce his allegiance to the basic socialist tenets. When questioned by the American authorities about the difference he made between Communism and Stalinism, he said that Stalinism meant slavery, hunger, and death, while Communism meant freedom and prosperity; this can hardly be viewed as a cautious reply to the official question whether he would want to spread Communism in the United States.

B. Behavior in the Interview

In the interviews M talked in a natural and animated way, without self-consciousness, easily responding to all questions and remarks and freely passing from one topic to another. He considered our tests something of a joke but went through them conscientiously, meeting the tester's apologies for imposing them on him with good-natured encouragement. In the more structured interviews M had no difficulty in sticking to the topic and discussing it coherently and fully; however, he obviously enjoyed the freedom offered by some of the clinical interviews where he was permitted to talk as he would in a conversation with friends. His language was rich and expressive, replete with vivid descriptions, with stories involving himself and others, with arguments and evaluations that were put forth clearly, personally, and concisely. The numerous concrete illustrations he adduced to make his points showed him to be an excellent observer and a realistic appraiser; they also revealed his enjoyment of the variety, color, and detail of the human panorama.

Along with the fluency of thought and expression, M displayed a wide range of moods and feelings depending on the topic discussed: sadness, worry, indignation, cheerful good humor, and a thorough enjoyment of humorous situations. All of these emotions appeared adequate, none were extreme, and he easily passed from one to another. During the study M was under a great deal of pressure, as his transactions with the American authorities did not proceed smoothly. He was impelled to discharge the bitter feelings of an uprooted and deprived man, and he frequently turned the interviews into counter-attacks on those who would brand as inferior the Russians, the Soviet people, or the DPs. Yet there was no sustained bitterness in these sallies and no rigid preconceptions; he frequently accepted, in a very genuine fashion, some point the interviewer would make to defend or to explain the people or the policies he was attacking, and his feelings changed accordingly. M could also be vigorously self-assertive about his feelings and views, though never unpleasantly. His emotions were expressed in such a way that they could be easily understood and shared by the interviewers; his frequent unrestrained laughter was contagious.

C. Relations to People

a. General Attitudes

M's great capacity for immediate emotional rapport with others manifested itself not only in free and pleasant interaction with the interviewers, regardless of differences of opinion; it was also obvious from his report of his past. One of the restrictions that had greatly irked him during his army career was the self-imposed limitations on sociability and hospitality which were dictated by caution. It was impossible to be frank with his colleagues; he felt he could completely trust only those friends who had gone through the Civil War with him. However, M's stories showed that he did not overdo caution; after his arrest even his prosecutors acknowledged that he was not, temperamentally, a conspirator. In the interviews, a great number of people of different classes and nationalities were mentioned by M as sources of information, or as witnesses who could confirm his observations and opinions: "a teacher of German whom we knew", "a forester who was in the camp with me", "a Jewish woman physician", "an old emigrant with whom I had an argument", "a soldier of mine, formerly a shoemaker", and many others; their experiences were related, sometimes even dramatically acted out, with the same vividness and immediacy as his own. He mentioned no particularly intimate friends, apart from his Civil War buddies, but his stories left no doubt that he had always had good friends and companions and that he would be very unhappy in isolation.

M's attitude to almost all of the people he mentioned was warm and sympathetic. He frequently expressed compassion for suffering, respect for integrity and "firm will", appreciation of competence, of artistic ability, of beauty and kindness in women; and he spoke tenderly about children. Even people whose actions aroused horror and indignation in him, and those who had caused his own suffering, were often discussed without bitterness. In many of his stories the persecutors were revealed as human; some of those who took children away from their parents during the collectivization cried as they did it, and some ended by committing suicide. A German general caught an escaping Russian prisoner of war; but, instead of having him shot, as was his duty, he gave him vodka and let him go. Slave laborers, upon liberation, were about to do away with their German landlord, but he asked their forgiveness—and obtained it. M himself was helped by the Americans to avoid the Repatriation Commission.

In talking about causation of human actions M showed a great deal of balance and common sense in seeing some of the causes in the person himself—his character, his nature— and some in the environmental inducements and pressures. However, he was not intent on disentangling psychological or other detail. When something in the person's behavior appeared incongruous, inexplicable as a response to the given situation, M was not interested in pursuing the problem in terms of hypothetical psychological reasons; he simply put it down to personal idiosyncrasy, perhaps constitutionally determined. But he was well aware of the impact of extreme situations. In talking about the irrational confessions obtained by Soviet investigators, he rejected the attempts—e.g., by Koestler—to explain them by the victim's basic identification with the ideology of his prosecutors. He saw these self-accusations as abnormal actions caused by an extreme abnormal situation. "Because the crime he is accused of is invented, his reactions also are twisted, abnormal. He tries to hold out, but he is being pushed to plunge into this world of fantasy; there is no way of dealing with it rationally. When he finally gives up and says the most awful things about himself, he may get a release of tension."

When the situations were within the normal range and the interplay of peoples' attitudes and actions was open to observation, M was quite capable of appreciating the psychological mechanisms involved—of seeing, e.g., how enduring attitudes may be formed in childhood, in the process of interaction with the family. Very frequently, in talking to us, he neither passed judgment on deviant or irrational behavior nor attempted to explain it; he simply enjoyed it, at least in retrospect, as another humorous example of human folly. He himself was tolerant of differences and felt that they need not endanger friendship and a feeling of fellowship. He participated in the polemics in the émigré press but reminded those of his friends who would let these issues cause personal enmities that if they wanted only one opinion to exist they need not have left the Soviet Union.

b. Parents and Children

M described his close relationships as having been always harmonious; this was true in his family. "Father had four brothers and three sisters, they were all close; I grew up in a patriarchal atmosphere of love and friendship." He characterized both parents as kind people, occasionally quoted his grandmother's shrewd sayings. His mother, he felt, was very tender and sympathetic to the children, although it was from her that he received the one beating of his childhood. He dwelt more on the personality of his father, with whom he seemed strongly identified. He depicted the father as a just man who was actively sympathetic and helpful to the members of the community and would even stand up for those whose misdeeds aroused the wrath of the majority. The children respected and obeyed him; they strove to live up to the standards of behavior and school achievement set by him, standards that were higher than those set for the other village children. "I remember how another boy first persuaded me to smoke, and I was terribly worried that father might find out. I was not afraid of punishment but of losing my parents' regard; they always told us we were better behaved than other children. I was the oldest and they paid more attention to my behavior; they felt I should be an example to the others."

M made his father's values his own and never lost his respect and affection for him, but these feelings did not prevent him from seeing the flaws in the upbringing he had received. "I

realized later that it would have been better if father had not
implanted this idea in me, this burden of pride; they should
have regarded us more democratically, as no different from
other children. As it was, I had to carry a great burden and
strive too hard. It might even have been better to be punished
by beatings, that is, treated like everybody else. I decided to
bring up my own child differently. I did not try to push and influence my daughter, to keep her on her toes. I think a child
can best develop her will if she does things on her own. I envied
my daughter for not being as burdened as I had been." M told
how his child would go to school cheerfully, without fear, even
if she had not prepared her lessons; he concluded that having
freed children from fear was an important achievement of the
Soviet school.

Whatever effects the early pressures had on M's mood and
development, they did not result in his isolating himself from
others through an assumed superiority. He not only held the
theory of people's basic equality but actually treated all people
as his equals. He also seemed to have no difficulties in relation
to people in authority and in exercising authority himself. He
must have been an excellent officer: straightforward, fair, firm
but not rigid in his demands and, beyond this, endearing himself to his men by his warm human response. In his educational
policies, both toward his child and his soldiers, he relied on personal example rather than on rules and maxims.

c. Women

M's relationship to women appeared only slightly more
problematic than that to men. He married at age thirty, as soon
as his external life became stabilized; before that he had had
many infatuations and many passing affairs. He described his
wife, who was ten years younger than he, in terms partly similar
to those he used for his mother: gentle, sympathetic, kind-
hearted almost to a fault. She relied on him for advice in all
important matters, and their life together was very harmonious,
based on mutual understanding and support. M approved of the
traditional distribution of roles between the two sexes, with the
man the breadwinner and head of the family, and the mother at
home with the children. This was how his family was run, ap-

parently to everyone's satisfaction. M did not invest these issues with any intense emotion, and his opinions were not rigid. He was willing and even eager for his daughter to study for a profession, feeling that this would make her more self-reliant, competent to take care of herself. In discussing the relationships between the sexes he never stressed the superiority theme and he was not threatened by the presence in their household of a rather domineering mother-in-law; having no trouble in asserting his wishes in all essential matters, he accepted her and appreciated her contribution to the household, in spite of his dislike for some of her traits.

M's descriptions of the comfort and pleasure he found at home sounded quite genuine, and his sorrow about the loss of his family was still acute. However, he made it fairly clear that his wife did not become the only woman in his life. He preferred to take his vacations without her, on hunting trips, or with army friends, and he hinted that he continued to be susceptible to feminine charm and did not always go out of temptation's way.

M experienced no serious guilt about his marital infidelities, actual or fantasied. When asked which impulses he found hard to suppress, he laughed and said that it would be embarrassing to talk about it; then he admitted that "woman plays a decisive role" in this topic, and that for a family man such impulses could be embarrassing. Probably as long as M could avoid embarrassment to himself and pain to his wife, he had no misgivings about enjoying an occasional affair, and felt about it as he did about premarital relations, namely that they were more excusable in men than in women; in a woman, he said, sex relations before marriage would indicate a greater lack of restraint and self-control. As a rationale for this double standard M would probably have cited the greater strength of the sex drive in men.

Without being at all censorious or intense, M was certain of the rightness of his opinions both about the standards of sexual behavior for the two sexes and about the best distribution of roles in the family. He felt that these opinions were shared by all classes of society in Russia. It is likely, however, that in this area he was more conservative than was the old intelligentsia; he seemed to adhere to the peasant tradition in a somewhat liberalized tolerant fashion.

d. Unconscious Dynamics

If we turn to the projective techniques for the elucidation of the unconscious dynamics underlying M's attitudes to men and women, we find evidence that his image of the ideal woman had two variants: that of a tender companion and that of an ardent lover. Such division could lead to conflicts and to unhappiness in relationships with women, but it did not seem to in his case. Probably one of the reasons for this happier outcome was that the split was not as radical as it could have been; the two roles were not those of a saint and a sinner, or of "spiritual" and "carnal" love. Both the tender and the erotic woman were perceived by M as very human, with no great gulf between them; at times the two conceptions came close to merging. In talking about the TAT picture of a young man and a young woman (Card 4) he decided that the girl was trying to keep the man, who had become interested in another. "She is very sweet, tender, hesitant; she does not grab him forcefully; she is troubled, uncertain of success." (How will it end? M laughs.) "She is also very beautiful; that counts, though it isn't true that beauty is all that matters; I can tell you that, I was a soldier and a bachelor for a long time, and I was often in love. . . .Perhaps if she makes an effort this sudden attraction for the other woman will pass. She is enchanting. She is not of those whom you would love with a sudden passion; your love for her would be less stormy, but all-absorbing. She has a high forehead, she is pleasing, and he is a person of strong will; such characters usually attract each other." Thus it seems that in M's eyes the ideal "tender" image also had an erotic component, even if the height of passion was to be reserved for less binding relationships.

The projective material and the "free associations", with which M's conversation abounded, give us some clues to the fantasies that possibly underlay the separation of eroticism from marriage. His projective stories depicted a close tender attachment to the mother, with a great deal of empathy and mutual dependence, and a partial continuation of the same type of relationship in marriage. There was some merging of the roles of mother and wife, but whenever an erotic feeling emerged, the wife in the stories changed into a mistress. The image of the father was that of a warm person, a good friend, yet there was also some anxiety that his firmness might turn into severity, and a suggestion of some issues between father and son that were not clear to the son. M's reaction to the TAT picture of an older and a younger man (Card 7) went, in part, as follows: "I don't know who it is. . .the young man is puzzled or astonished, the older one has told him something that surprised him . . .or else they are both puzzled, I can't get it. . . .Yes, both puzzle over something. . .they are struck by some event, not a pleasant one. . . (What could it be?). Something about a person who is close to them, an action they did not expect. . .something about a relative, wife, or mother, or sister. (Are these two related?) They seem like father and son in age, though there is not much resemblance; they are close, they don't restrain their expression. (What will they do?) They are momentarily puzzled . . . .I don't know what the painter had in mind; too bad there are no captions!" (He laughs.)

The unclear issue may possibly have pertained to the mother. It should be noted that the only concrete story involving his father that M told in the interview was about his standing up for a woman caught in adultery; this had impressed his son as very noble and generous. Possibly the young man of his fantasy was uncertain whether the father would be understanding and tolerant of his feelings toward the mother, or angered and jealous; whether or not he would want to separate them. It will be remembered that in his childhood M resented his father's insistence on better behavior and higher achievement partly because it threatened to separate him from his social environment in the village. He may also have feared that his pursuing this course would create a gulf between him and his mother who was less educated than his father; in the son's mind she was identified—as his "free associations" abundantly show—with village and peasantry. Under these conditions it would be natural for the boy to interpret the father's pressure for higher education and status as a wish to separate him from the comforts of home and from his mother. These fears had to be handled in some way, particularly as they seemed to be born out by reality; going to high school actually necessitated M's leaving home at an early age.

Despite these conflicts M proved able to achieve a solid identification with his father and with the male role, while preserving an affectionate relationship with his mother, and later with his wife. Perhaps this achievement was facilitated by his developing the belief that the turbulent "intense passions" had no place within the family and should be kept outside its confines. This, of course, is no more than a conjecture, with only a limited material to support it. Whatever the origins of M's sentiments about women, his generally harmonious relationships with both sexes indicate that any pressures he had been subject to as a child were far outweighed by the benign features of his environment; his appraisal of the parental directions as clear cut and of the family atmosphere as basically friendly and harmonious must have been essentially correct. Under these conditions the incompletely resolved childhood conflicts are not likely to lead to the development of a pervasive neurosis.

e. Insight into Self

As noted before, in his relationships with people M showed a sound, if unsophisticated, appreciation of emotional motivation and a tolerant acceptance of human weakness. The same capacity for insight and acceptance was shown in his attitude toward himself. By and large, he lived up to his ideals of honesty, objectivity, and self-control, and he had an adequate regard for himself. When at times he was caught, or caught himself, in a deviation from this responsible rational course, he had no great difficulty in seeing the real motive behind his act or thought and admitting it to himself and to others.

Once during an interview M was holding forth about the prospects for a quick capitulation of the Soviet regime in case of war or of Stalin's death, and the interviewer remarked on his optimism. He laughed and said that a friend of his had also asked him whether he really believed in such an eventuality; then he admitted that he was perhaps a drowning man grasping at a straw: "Because if I did not believe it, what would I have to live by?" He made several other admissions of wishful thinking, or wishful blindness, in talking about his reactions to various upsetting events in the Soviet Union. In discussing a projective episode involving a conflict between honesty and doing a favor to a friend, M started by strongly advocating honesty, which was a part of his code of honor; soon, however, he spontaneously admitted that in the case of a good friend, or of one who would not take no for an answer, he would give him a noncommittal recommendation; he himself characterized such acts as "formally correct but essentially deceitful". Asked about his reason for this decision, he did not take refuge in the competing value of helping friends but laughed and said: "Our relationships are often built on compromise; one just doesn't feel like making enemies unnecessarily—what for? If you refuse him, he may turn against you." Whenever he admitted in this way some reprehensible motives he usually took it as a good joke on himself and as a demonstration of the fact that "we are all human, after all".

D. Ideology of Equality

M's personal ideology must be fairly clear to the reader by now; to give a full review of it seems unnecessary. He, himself, summarized some of its main points when he told us that he had wanted to bring up his child to love her work, to be honest with herself and frank with others, to love, trust and obey her parents, and to develop to the full her artistic abilities. (M was very fond of music and poetry and frequently quoted songs and poems.) The essential point in assessing his personality is that his ideals were in harmony with his own inclinations and that he strove to live up to them, even while realizing that he could not be perfect and always succeed. We shall dwell at length only on one part of his ideology, his emphasis on the equality of all people. This sentiment was similar to M's other beliefs in being felt strongly and personally, but the intensity he showed in defending it was a unique feature suggesting that this one belief might also serve some other function than the expression of a personal ideal. The adjustive or defensive features of M's belief in equality seem to be connected with his attitude to the Soviet regime.

The equality about which M felt so strongly was not the equality of opportunities, or of material benefits, of physical comforts. He sympathized with the deprived and the suffering and considered this sympathy to be a natural human response; but he told us that on this score he did not feel as strongly as, e.g., his wife, who cried at the sight of a beggar; he disapproved of her intensity. His own feelings, however, were raised to a high pitch whenever people were disparaged, denied the value and dignity of human beings as such, their basic equality with others. Hitler's doctrine of the "Untermensch" with no claim to respect and human treatment, the willfulness of the old Russian merchants, the haughtiness of the aristocracy toward the "rabble" who presumably had no pride and felt no humiliation, and, most of all, the presumption of the old intelligentsia in believing themselves to be morally and intellectually superior to the people whom they wanted to "serve", all these postures of superiority filled M with hot indignation. In opposing them he took up the defense of the simple Russian people as possessing excellent insight and common sense, as having a reservoir of inner strength for shaping their common destinies and affecting the destinies of the world.

The strong emotion displayed by M in attacking all those who would devalue and degrade others never turned against the Soviet regime. He asserted that, all the misuse of power notwithstanding, the regime had lived up to its original intention to abolish the differences between social classes; it had, in fact, fostered egalitarian attitudes, the "democracy of everyday life", as he called it, even while doing away with all democratic procedures. In talking about his willingness to do manual labor M had this to say: "With us in the Soviet Union any work is considered noble. . .the old émigrés have lost contact with Russia; they think our revolution has been imported from outside in a suitcase; this is not so, it grew from inside. The émigrés have not changed, but Russia has. A democratization has taken place; nobody is astonished now when a worker marries a woman doctor. There is cruelty, terror, much that is ugly and distorted, but nobody can feel any longer that he is better than another. After all, one keeps telling the simple people that they are the boss, and actually outside prisons and camps, no one is permitted to hit or insult a worker. The upper classes are hard pressed, but the workers' dignity has been raised; true, he can be executed, but as long as he is free he is the equal of anyone. When the Germans subjected peasants to corporal punishment, the national feeling of the whole village was offended."

M realized, of course, the existence of material inequality in the Soviet Union. He deplored the general lack of economic security, gave dramatic examples of people whose subsistence level was close to starvation, and admitted that after collectivization the peasants were much worse off than before. He found ways, however, to minimize the role of differential earnings in positing the superiority of one group over another, in creating class distinctions and breeding resentment. "Material advantages are earned by hard work and they are his only as long as he works on the job. Tomorrow they may be someone else's; this softens the feeling of class envy. The gulf between the classes has been filled in, even if this was done with endless sacrifices and bloodshed." M abhorred the cruelty and heartlessness of the regime, but the presumed achievement of doing away with inequality was more important to him. One may wonder if he did not speak for himself when he mused about history's judgment about Stalin: "I wonder if history will justify his deeds. They are frightening even to think about, they evoke such hatred. . . .But history is kind; it has even justified Ivan the Terrible for the crimes he committed in founding the empire."

True to his essentially realistic perceptions, M did not drastically distort the facts on which his evaluations were based; yet in some of his arguments the tendency to maximize the newly achieved dignity of the Soviet people and to minimize the existing drastic class differences was quite striking. Even more striking was his complete silence about the fact that collectivization and other repressive policies of the regime had resulted in the creation of a new "lower class" of disadvantaged people, much less "equal" than all others. (How the members of the latter group perceived the Soviet "classless society" was shown by one respondent of low education who said that what he liked best in Germany was the absence of social classes; it turned out that he meant the absence of legally disadvantaged groups like the "kulaks" and their descendants.) M showed a similar bias on many minor points. For example, in telling of his avoidance of

DP camps, he said that even standing in line for food hurt a proud person's dignity. He went on to discuss how the people's feeling of self-respect had been fostered by the "everyday democracy of Soviet life", without giving any thought to the amount of time the ordinary Soviet citizens spent standing in lines, and how this affected their dignity.

These conspicuous omissions of pertinent points, and the selective levelling and sharpening of facts, confirm the assumption that M had a special investment in the "equality" aspect of his ideology. The high value he placed on equality helped him to justify to himself and to others his own course in life, including his former support of the Soviet regime. The necessity for self-defense was probably felt by M more strongly than usual in the situation of being questioned by Americans, but this need may also have had roots in his own misgivings about his actions. M's descriptions of his childhood suggest the possible origins of these misgivings.

In spite of his strong feeling of belongingness with the village children, M did strive successfully to be better than they in achievement and behavior, in order to please his father. He remained singularly free of feelings of superiority, becoming neither overbearing nor condescending, but he did join the elite and enjoyed prestige and material advantages out of reach of the "masses". When the life of the peasantry was being ravaged by collectivization, he found himself allied with the persecutors of the group that had had his earliest allegiance; this was probably the main source of guilt in his life. It is no wonder that he "lost touch" with the village life after the collectivization and that he was eager to find signs of beneficent changes in the villages; such changes would prove that all the suffering had not been in vain. When M once again found himself among the defenseless who could be scorned with impunity, his early identification with the downtrodden and the despised came to the fore and he vigorously denounced the maligners of the "common people".

Thus, the ideological issues that engaged M's emotions can be seen as reflecting his early problem of double identification, with the downtrodden people and with the elite, a problem possibly linked to his early relationship with his parents. In the process of partially renouncing the close tie of the firstborn to his mother, for the sake of growing up and being approved by his father, M must have experienced both resentment and guilt. The conflict could be resolved and these feelings could be kept in abeyance while he was allied with the leadership that he felt took to heart the people's interests. Such an opportunity had been afforded him for a long time by his service in the Red Army; it gave meaning to his life and contributed to making his mature years happy and productive. This is probably why, after the Soviet government proved to be cruel and repressive and did indeed separate M from "Mother Russia", he still clung to the belief that the good it did for the Russian people was not outweighed by the bad. His attitude might have been different if he had been younger and if some new and better leadership had been in sight; he might have been able to ally himself with it, just as he had once replaced the liberal intelligentsia by Lenin. This leadership, however, would have had to be Russian. In talking about the democracy of the West, M quoted the saying "she is fine, but she is not mine"; he would probably have had the same feeling even if the "democracy" had been as kind to the DPs as he wished it to be. M had been a great admirer of the popular military heroes of the Soviets; had they actually started an armed uprising at the time when his disillusionment had progressed far enough, he might have joined with enthusiasm. In the absence of "own" leadership, he could not have thrown himself wholeheartedly into the anti-Soviet fight even if offered a chance. Unlike many other DPs, he showed no eagerness to get into this fight, to direct or advise Western action, especially military action against Russia. This lack of a "cause", this impossibility to ally himself at least internally with a course promising to return him to Russia, contributed to his resignation; he felt that real meaningful life had ended for him.

E. Sources of Strength and Weakness

In conclusion, we shall briefly review the sources of strength and weakness in M's personality structure. Let it be said at once that the balance was definitely on the side of strength. M was given a rating of better than average adjustment; he was one of the soundest members of the group we studied. We felt that he combined great emotional spontaneity and expressiveness with a sound grasp of reality, a control based on awareness, sound and effective ideals and a capacity to work persistently for long-range goals. The healthy organization was clearly predominant in M's personality. Its predominance was not seriously threatened even by the discouraging situation he found himself in, with its lack of essential satisfactions and few hopes for the future. This situation made his shortcomings more pronounced, but the main outlines of his enduring personality organization remained clearly visible across his reactions to frustration.

Let us now turn to these weaknesses. A closer look at M's mechanisms of control shows them to be imperfect. They were neither rigid nor brittle but their effectiveness varied and they did not always work without fail. He was considered by others, and considered himself, as lacking in restraint at times. Under extreme frustration he would often flare up in anger; after having had to suppress his annoyance at work, he would burst out in curses as soon as he entered his apartment, so that his daughter learned to run and close all windows whenever he came home in a bad mood. Possibly he also had had to fight the tendency to work in spurts, with great expenditure of energy followed by periods of discouragement. This pattern was indicated in the Rorschach Test and in the TAT where, after a vigorous start, he would respond to the rising pressure of fantasies by almost deliberately stopping the flow, and after a while his productivity would go down. This pattern of "giving up" may have been intensified by the mild resignation of a man who felt he had lived his life, who had little hope of regaining his former sources of satisfaction or developing new ones.

However, neither emotional outbursts nor lasting discouragement were typical of M's way of handling frustrating situations. The projective techniques and the reports of his past indicated that difficulties usually spurred him on to renewed efforts, to deliberate attempts to master the situation by understanding and by his own ingenuity. At times he would seek help, at times reject it—if his pride and stubbornness were aroused—but basically he dealt with problems in a self-reliant fashion and admired those who find their way out of difficult situations. In his own career the pleasure in learning, in increasing his competence through the discipline of training and work, had been quite marked. M may have been handicapped in fully developing his intelligence and competence by his relative lack of interest in detail. He professed a dislike for routine, and his intellectual approach to problems (as shown both in the Rorschach and in his conversation) was characterized by a large overview and good common sense. His thinking was in close touch with reality, but it was neither abstract nor very precise. Typically, he admired those thinkers who, like Lenin, could clearly articulate "the vague conceptions and feelings" of many people. He himself did not feel capable of mastering complex phenomena intellectually. Much of the concrete detail of his experience was reserved by him for aesthetic and empathic appreciation rather than for intellectual analysis.

The picture of M as revealed by the projective techniques was quite consistent with his manifest personality, but it placed relatively more emphasis on his childlike qualities: his gentleness, his vulnerability, and his wish for affectionate support. Some of his actual hotheadedness, stubbornness, and determination could be viewed as his ways of counteracting these softer, yielding aspects of his nature; the alternation of vigorous warm outgoingness with resigned withdrawal may have been due to fear of hurt. Yet there was no deep split between these different tendencies; the fact that he was able to accept and integrate them to an astonishing degree, with a minimum of distortion, was an outstanding characteristic of M's personality structure. Much of the repressed content of his mind was not very far from the surface; when it became disturbing it was pushed back almost deliberately. Thus, in the Rorschach Test, after having revealed some interest in body functions through his associations to one of the blots, he put the card away after one response, saying: "Let it go, I better put it away quickly, so it won't trouble me any more."

This attitude seemed to be typical of M's dealings with disturbing unconscious or partly conscious fantasies. He knew intuitively of their existence, was partly aware of the anxiety they generated, and tolerated it up to a point. When these states became too disturbing, he put them away and went on with the business in hand; this deliberate suppression was in line with his philosophy of rational self-control. Such a policy may have prevented him from utilizing his fantasies for internal creativeness, but it kept them sufficiently accessible to permit their free infusion into a personal response to the outside world, which made him such a colorful figure. In this fluid expressive response he shared and socialized his fantasies, alleviating his anxiety also by such devices as humor and jokes. Free emotional interchange with others was both the true medium of M's personal creativeness and a means of assimilating disturbances and anxieties. This strong need for interchange did not lead to submissive dependence on others, as was clearly shown by M's behavior in the interrogation; under the pressure of fantastic accusations and threats he resisted vigorously and successfully the temptation to become submerged in the irrational thinking, to be caught in the "net of lies". His internal strength and resiliency were demonstrated by the whole course of his life; even after having lost all that had been most meaningful to him, and saddened by this forced premature "retirement", he was neither disorganized nor bitter.

Chapter 2

ALEXEI—A SKILLED WORKER

A. Life History

Alexei, a thirty-two-year-old skilled worker of peasant origin (born in 1918), had no record of repression in the Soviet Union and was quite favorable to the regime. He was an officer in the Red Army when he was taken prisoner by the Germans in 1942; he immediately decided not to return, soberly anticipating punishment for this "betrayal of his country". After liberation he married a Russian girl, another displaced person. At the time of the study they were living in a DP camp and were being processed for immigration to the United States, with good chances of success.

a. Childhood and Adolescence

A grew up in a village in central Russia, the second of three sons of a middle peasant; up to the time of collectivization the family, though not well off, suffered no severe hardships. A felt that during his childhood he "took in strength" which stood him in good stead during later periods of privation. From his simple narrative about the events of his early life, A emerged as an alert, active child, very sociable, striving to command other children, and freely participating in their games, mischief, and fights. He described his parents as very good to the children and none too strict. He got occasional beatings from his mother, which he did not seem to resent. In telling about it he said, "A mother is a mother" and quoted a Russian saying: "She cuffs you and she loves you." A talked more about his father, who never punished the children but who definitely had their respect: "I knew what he told me was right; if he just gave me a stern look I knew. . . ." It was the father who set the goals for the children; he wanted them to get more education than he himself had had and to learn a skill, so that they could escape

59

the hard life of a peasant. He saw to it that they did their
schoolwork, saying that they would be grateful to him later on.

Father also provided companionship. A enjoyed listening to
his stories of old times, of the hardships the father had suffered
growing up in a large peasant family. In later years he loved to
go hunting with him and with his older brother. He recalls quar-
reling with this brother when he would not take him along; A
would steal gunpowder from him and the brother would beat
him up. These defeats were partly compensated by the allegiance
of his younger brother of whom he was very fond. A sometimes
envied the children of the richer families who had more access
to entertainment; once he asked his father why he could not
have what they had. By and large, however, his early childhood
memories were happy and did not suggest severe pressures.

The same was true of his life in school. It was easy for A to
accept and fulfill his parents' wishes concerning schooling; being
of a curious bent of mind he went to school eagerly, learned
rapidly, and was among the best students. He fully believed
what he was taught about life in the Soviet Union, i.e., that it
was much better than life abroad and than life before the
revolution; this was consistent with his father's tales of the past.
On the other hand, the school did not succeed in explicitly
turning A against religion, because, as he said, "How could I
deny what my parents believed?" However, as the parents offered no religious instruction and the churches were closed, this
was of little practical consequence; religion had not acquired
any personal meaning for A and had not become a cause of discord between him and the new social order. As the peasants
during the NEP period were not in opposition to the regime,
there was no conflict for him between home and school; in fact,
he must have felt their goals to be quite harmonious.

The period of collectivization disrupted this harmony. A's
father at first resisted joining the kolkhoz, and in retaliation all
his property, including his only cow, was taken away. He appealed this action first to the local authorities and then by
letter to Kalinin, titular chief of state. Eventually a reply came
which the family considered favorable, but the local authorities
did not act on it; the father had to give in and join the kolkhoz.
They were economically worse off for having attempted resist-

ance, but they escaped being permanently branded as "enemies", and their life was not disrupted at first as was that of the de-kulakized peasants. A recalled witnessing with consternation the uprooting of his friends and their wanderings in search of shelter and work. Soon his own turn came to go off. Famine struck the depleted village, and the family, with its reduced resources, barely escaped starvation. A, at the age of fourteen, found his way to the coal region of the Donbas; he spent some time working in the mines and then returned home to work in the kolkhoz. These were the years of privation; all his wishes and dreams were of earnings that would permit him to get enough food, to buy shoes and clothes.

b. Youth and Adulthood

A turn for the better came when young peasants were encouraged to apply for technical training. A spent two years in a trade school in the nearby city, and was then employed as a skilled worker in an armaments factory. The four years he spent on this job before being drafted into the army (age 20 to 24) were the happiest of his life. He was good at his work and he loved it; he was in congenial company, with people of the same background as his; he earned relatively well and was satisfied with his lot.

Although A was well oriented both in the official and unofficial structure of the plant and was able to "pull the ropes" to his advantage, his ambition for bettering himself had very definite limits. He did not want to be pushed into a position of greater responsibility, always dangerous, and he did not want to lose the friendship of his co-workers, most of whom, being peasants' sons, were either indifferent or hostile to the Party. For these reasons he steadfastly resisted the pressure for joining the Komsomol (the communist youth organization), giving the usual reason of "unworthiness", and carefully saw to it that his work output was good but not outstanding. A's older brother had chosen a different course; at the end of his term in the army, when faced with the choice of either returning to the misery of the kolkhoz or entering an NKVD (secret police) school, he chose the latter; he tried to persuade A to join the Party for the sake of his career. A passed no judgment on his brother; he felt that many of those who joined the Party in order to "improve their life" remained good men, not domineering or supercilious toward non-Party people. Others, however, did pester and even denounce their comrades. A shared the common mistrust and dislike of Party members as potential disruptors; their presence divided the workers into two groups, while he "wanted all of us to be as one".

Despite this mistrust and his hearty dislike of the pretense and pressure of such institutions as the sessions of "self-criticism" and the "socialist competition", A felt by no means inimical toward the regime. He was never, in his adult life, helplessly exposed to its pressures. He found ways to protect himself against all attempts to extract the maximum efforts from the workers. We heard from him and from many others that workers in the Soviet plants preferred to keep to themselves the little tricks and improvements they invented to make their work faster and easier. If the invention was not sufficiently important to bring them financial rewards, these secrets protected them from being crushed by excessive demands. A had figured out one such improvement; as the sole possessor of this "secret", he was able to fulfill the norm with less effort and rush. He had also found ways to resist the pressure for extensive financial contributions; he maintained, e.g., that he had managed to avoid membership in a trade union, having figured out that the probable benefits did not balance the dues. Belonging to unions was obligatory; very few succeeded in staying out.

Having avoided the worst pressures, A felt that the state had treated him well in enabling him to learn a skill, to use it, and to improve his material condition. A trip to Latvia and Lithuania with a workers' excursion made him realize the better conditions of life abroad and the unreliability of the Soviet press; but, in view of his basic satisfaction with his lot, these discoveries did not undermine his loyalty. The German invasion fanned his patriotic feelings, and the death of his favorite younger brother made him want to wreak vengeance on the enemy. Called into the army, he went through a wartime officers' school and after six months at the front was taken prisoner. He told of fighting to the last moment, then yielding to a friend's plea not to have them all slaughtered and permitting the men to surrender or to run. He himself tried to escape but was overtaken and captured. Then and there he decided not to return, feeling that, as an officer, he could expect no clemency from his government. He criticized rather mildly the regime's stand expressed in the infamous "Stalin's law": "The last bullet is for yourself." "If I had put down arms," he said, "and refused to defend my country, then I agree I should be shot, but in such circumstances, when nothing more could be done, how can you expect a human being to stop wanting to live and to kill himself?"

As a prisoner of war A suffered severe privations and his health was undermined. Soon after his liberation and his marriage he developed tuberculosis and had to spend three years in a sanitarium. After his discharge he found work on a German farm; the farmer's family appreciated him greatly because of the wide range of his skills, from mechanical repairs to baking. A enjoyed having their regard but did not fail to rub in the lesson which he felt they must learn about Russians. Being naturally fastidious, he would ostentatiously abstain from eating if he noticed any impurity in the food, and then remark that Russians were not "Untermenschen" or pigs. In spite of his good life on the farm, A soon began to long for Russian companionship and, with his wife, moved to a DP camp. In the camp it was more difficult to earn one's living and he often worried about the morrow, but he was happier among his own. At the time of the interviews his wife was expecting a child, and A was overjoyed about it. He was planning to join friends who had preceded him to the United States; he was fairly well informed about conditions there and quite realistic in his expectations. His dreams were of economic security rather than great prosperity. Though he hoped eventually to do the skilled work for which he had been trained, he expected rough going at first and was prepared to take any job.

Like most displaced persons, A expressed great longing for Russia; unlike many others, however, he did not daydream of returning. Perhaps because he had no real animus against the regime, he did not dwell on the idea of overthrowing it by military intervention; apparently he considered this as unlikely as internal collapse. He would not have hesitated to return to the Soviet Union if he could have been certain of his safety; however, the situation being what it was, he had clearly put Russia into the past and oriented himself to the future in the New World. After having told, with great sympathy, about a friend who had proved unable to bear the lonely life outside Russia, A said that he himself did not give up and hoped to build a new life for himself in America: "My hope is that there are good people everywhere, that they will understand us and help us; and we will prove our gratitude, just give us time."

B. Behavior in the Interview

In the interviews A displayed an outgoing vigorous response, a thorough involvement in the topics under discussion, combined with a full measure of control. He talked freely and fluently, giving his narratives a vivid emotional coloring, but at no time, in no mood, did he pour out his feelings, and he was never carried away by his story or his arguments. Although he did say with feeling that the happy periods in his life had been short and few, that he had had no time to enjoy his youth, he did not dwell on the harrowing experiences that had been his lot. He told only in passing that at home they ate grass during the famine and were all swollen up; that as a prisoner he was severely beaten by the Germans. In telling about the happy aspects of his life, such as his marriage and his expected child, A at times became quite eloquent, but he never sounded boastful or exuberant. Through all the variations of mood and topics, he always appeared as a person who had both feet firmly on the ground. He, himself, explicitly expressed his aversion to false and exaggerated emotions, when telling about the irrational behavior he had observed at a meeting of some religious sect: "It is repulsive to see how they beat their heads and to hear them shriek; they use religion as a pretext to drive themselves into madness."

While maintaining his generally composed mood, A kept up a high level of energy throughout the interviews, with no marked ups or downs. Whether the topic demanded a narration of past events, an expression of beliefs and opinions, or a free play of fantasy, he tackled it without hesitation in a matter-of-fact way and did a good job of each task. He expressed his sentiments with conviction, pleasantly gave free rein to fantasy in projective techniques, and was sound and moderate in his observations and judgments. Particularly impressive in a person who had finished only seven grades of school was the unpretentious but serious effort he made, in response to the questions on ideology, to develop a full and coherent philosophy of human life in society. His thesis that "man should develop on all sides: communistically, democratically and spiritually" and that the government must serve all these purposes, while it lacked in discussion of instrumentalities, was an impressive attempt at an intellectual synthesis of genuine personal convictions. At the same time, this thesis, insisting as it did on equal development of man's different trends, stressed the value of sound balance, which characterized A's own behavior.

C. Relations to People

a. Interaction

As to the actual content of A's strivings, we found most outstanding his great need and wish for the company of friends, for social interaction, for belongingness. He founded and maintained a family against great odds in exile, he repeatedly sacrificed material advantages to this need for company and friendship; in telling about every crucial moment of his past he mentioned some friends who had shared his vicissitudes, plans and decisions. The same stress on interactive process appeared in A's responses to projective techniques; his TAT stories dealt mostly with relationships; the concerns and hopes he discussed in the Projective Questions referred to situations involving other people; he did a superlative job on the "Episodes" which demand solution of interpersonal problems. The interview itself was often transformed by A into a conversation; he not only told about himself and expressed his own views but also inquired, in a very natural way, about the life history and the opinions of the interviewer and freely responded to the information given. As a result of this conversational nature of the interview, large parts of it had to be written down after A had left; he had no objections to our note-taking, but he talked with real feeling and participation only as long as he could hold the other person's eye and talk directly to her; the moment the interviewer looked at her notes, his speech lost the natural animation and expressiveness of real communication. Consequently, she often abstained from note-taking; some of A's most vivid stories were not recorded verbatim.

A did not limit the interchange with the project members to the interview situation. He extended the relationship further, by inviting one of his male interviewers and his wife to visit him in his camp. When the late hour made their return to the city difficult, he offered them hospitality for the night, the hosts sharing their only room with the guests.

b. Equality and Unity

A treated the interviewers as equals, without subservience or embarrassment; this was his usual approach to people, and it was reflected in his ideology of universal equality, which he asserted as a matter of course, with no personal intensity.

A's freedom from discriminatory attitudes was manifested quite consistently whether he talked about races, nationalities, religions, social classes, or Party and non-Party people. These categories as such had no value connotations for him and not much "existential" reality. He said he preferred Russians to the Germans as being "always in a good mood, more giving and hospitable", but apart from this he was at a loss to find any essential differences between various nationalities he had known. When questioned the only thing he was able to say about the Ukrainians was that they wore their national dress on holidays; and about the Jews, that they were a "believing people" whose holiday was Saturday instead of Sunday. He de-emphasized the differences that he knew to exist. Though quite alert to the differences in material status and fully aware that the peasants were worse off than the workers, he showed no interest in differentiating between the social classes on this or any other basis. He stressed that, except for those repressed by the regime, all people in the Soviet Union had equal opportunities, because all had access to education, and that all classes were equally "basic".

A's attitudes were realistic enough, even if, in part, they embodied his personal wishes. He acknowledged the existence of differences and groupings among people, was mildly interested in them, but deplored the fact that they often created segregation and strife. He strongly advocated religious freedom and would let everyone believe as he would, but since religious differences could lead to disunity and discord he wished they did not exist.

In the Projective Questions A gave a striking expression to his feelings by formulating his "impossible wish" thus: "To unite the whole world into one and have only one language, so that wherever you went everyone would understand you, and there would be no racial or chauvinistic opinions." In spite of all the obstacles to communication, A himself had persistently pursued his wish to "unite with everybody". Not being hampered by any preconceptions, he seemed to approach all people with the hope of establishing a companionable relationship, or at least of exploring this possibility. If the other's attitudes or actions frustrated his wish, he accepted this with a measure of equanimity, because, he said, "I can always find another who has a better understanding of things." All the evidence indicated that A had experienced little difficulty in having his wish for companionship constantly and adequately satisfied.

What specific satisfactions did A desire and obtain through the medium of companionship? We shall try to identify various trends within this complex of "social satisfactions".

c. Recognition and Acceptance

A wished to be liked, to be approved by others, to be given recognition, to have their regard. He cited with pleasure instances of obtaining this satisfaction. In all these episodes recognition was earned by competence, such as quickly solving a difficult technical problem in his work. As a child he had wished he could be a national hero like Chapayev; the decision he made during the war to enlist in an aviation school was determined in part by the general popularity of pilots; he felt his courage and his resourcefulness to be adequate to the demands of this heroic job. A was quite frank with us about his wish for recognition. In answering the projective question concerning his wishes for his son, he utilized fully and with relish the freedom from all realistic limitations: "I would like him to be a prominent international athlete, or a national singer of great popularity; as a third wish, I wish that he would be an outstanding courageous hero, like Suvorov or Kutuzov, and that his fame would spread in the whole world; or else a scientific genius who would discover something new for the people."

Yet A's reply to another projective question expressed his feeling that a wish for supreme fame could be dangerous if it became the dominant passion, compelling the person to over-reach himself and to lose touch with others: "A person could also become insane if he is a scientific worker who wants to become a genius, an outstanding person; if he has to deal with a lot of contradictions in the literature of his field and cannot solve them, he may eventually go insane, if he should throw away all other wishes for the sake of science."

In his actual conduct of life A seemed to subordinate his desire for wide recognition to his wish for the goodwill and approval of people with whom he was closely associated. In discussing the reasons why an adult son should not push his views against the parents' opposition, he said: "If I did, their regard for me would change; they would feel that I refused them obedience, and in their community they might suffer shame through me." It would have grieved him, he said, if his parents had lost confidence in him "as their devoted son". He actually gave up his pilot's training at the insistence of his mother, who was concerned for his safety and appealed to his feeling for her.

A's wish to keep the confidence and regard of others was very strong in relation to friends and co-workers. In discussing the situation of a man whose friends seem secretly displeased with him, he said that this man would labor under a heavy burden, that "he must find out why they despise him and settle this conflict; there must be frankness, otherwise it will affect his personal life". He, himself, had consistently acted in accordance with this idea. When some of his compatriots suspected him of some wrongdoing, he did not rest until he had proved his innocence. Once a German employer, over his protests, put him into a better job, displacing another man; when A discovered that the other workers resented this, he insisted on returning to his former job.

In spite of this great wish for people's regard, A did not appear enslaved to this wish. Though fantasying world fame, in reality he had not been too concerned about how he was viewed by people to whom he was not close, or not tied by the situation. A man disliked by his co-workers, he said, could "go to another place, where he could develop friendlier feelings toward others, and they toward him". Even with people whose regard was important for him, he was not apt to disguise his opinions for the sake of approval; he felt that if he had something to say he would say it, no matter who was listening. Nor would he take another's opinion against his better knowledge. Pleased as he was with his friends' high opinion of his marriage, he said that, no matter what they thought, he and his wife had their unavoidable share of troubles, and proceeded to describe them. He felt quite free to disagree and argue with the interviewer; he did not seem intent on pleasing her.

All of this indicates that while A wanted people's regard, his own self-concept and self-respect were not dependent on it. Apparently people's liking and esteem were essential not for raising his self-confidence but as necessary preconditions for a companionable relationship, for shared membership in a group. It is interesting to note that, of all the achievements that can bring fame, A dwelt most on those of great singers and dancers, whom he admired wholeheartedly. (Russians do not share the Americans' feeling that professional dancing is only for effeminate men; ballet dancers are felt to be strong and manly.) He, himself, played the accordion in his youth; in his TAT story about the boy with the violin he said that if the hero succeeded in mastering the instrument he would be popular among his friends. Thus, fame was visualized by A not as an abstract and distant tribute to superior performance (as, e.g., in honoring scientists) but as an audience's immediate response to the artist who brings them pleasure.

d. Leadership and Understanding

A's sentiments about leadership showed similar features. He had obviously been a good officer during his brief military career and had had no misgivings about exercising authority. Yet, he showed no evidence of any wish to lead or to dominate people. He completed the sentence fragment: "To lead people ..." with the words "is prideful", instead of the usual reference to the difficulties and responsibilities of leadership; this response is understandable in the light of his experience with the Party members who placed themselves above the other workers and tried to "enlighten" them. A named Lenin as his admired hero, but in discussing him and his other heroes he did not stress the aspect of leading or influencing people. He expressed admiration for a strong person's ability to reach his goals in the face of obstacles, he felt awed by scientific discoveries which show "how highly the human being is developed, what ability and strength of purpose he has", but essentially he emphasized what the great man does *for* the people, and the love and admiration he receives in return. In contrasting Stalin with Lenin, who he felt had planned to achieve collectivization gradually and with the people's consent, he expressed his dislike for domination and coercion.

A definite if inconspicuous component in A's enjoyment of company was *curiosity*. He was curious about the world in general and had a childlike eagerness for new experiences and for adventure. When his imagination was given free rein by the projective question about three impossible things, he mentioned the wish to fly to Mars to see what this other world looked like. Mostly, however, his curiosity was directed toward people and their various ways of life. In the Soviet Union he had frequently wished he could visit other places and other factories; he would have loved to make a trip around the world; the prohibition of foreign travel was one of his complaints against the regime. He frankly expressed his curiosity about the interviewer and questioned her about her life history and her opinions.

Though perhaps childlike and naive, A's curiosity was not mere "idle" curiosity. He was not given to detailed analyses of people, but he definitely wanted to understand them, to know the reasons for their actions, because "there can be no companionship without mutual understanding". In discussing (in the Episodes) the situation of a foreman worried about decreasing production, A had this to say in favor of understanding: "He must discuss with them the reasons that prevent them from raising production; perhaps it is their economic situation at home, or they are displeased with something, maybe he himself has been rude to them. He should stop and think and ask himself: how do I stand with them? Perhaps they want to have me replaced by another. . .there is no use to try and talk them into working harder. . .you have to find the reason, the cause."

e. Support

Besides wanting people's regard, and wanting to understand them, A also wanted from them help and support, material and emotional comforts. This wish strongly colored his attitude to his wife and was often expressed with frank naiveté. He told us that during his stay in the sanitarium his wife had worked and struggled to be able to bring him additional food. He described her as a good housekeeper: "In the morning she has everything ready, my clothes and all; she sees me off properly. . .and she feels for me, as a wife should. . .if I as much as get a cold she is worried." Both in the projective techniques and in talking about himself, A repeatedly mentioned concern about the absence or loss of this support: "When my wife is ill I worry and wonder if it might be serious. The thought comes to me that if she fell ill and went to a hospital, I would have a hard time doing everything myself. A single man in emigration has a hard time. . .who will wash and cook for you?"

The connection between being loved and being fed was quite strong in A's mind. Even outside of the relationship to maternal women, he frequently referred to food, both in the passive and in the active context. Asked about the best jobs in the Soviet Union, he named jobs in provisionment, where a person can "fix himself up" with food. On the other hand, the wish to give also made him think of food. Asked about his friendships in the Soviet Union, he said: "In other countries you can probably do more for your friends, you can get them good things to eat. But what could we do? Just give a friend a glass of vodka or a slice of tomato. But our hearts were warm just the same." Sitting at table, drinking and talking, played a prominent part in A's idea of a happy reunion with friends. Hospitable himself, he enjoyed the role of host. He actually brought wine, bread, and sausage to an interview and insisted that the interviewer eat and drink with him. The issue of drinking did not loom large in A's life. He did not drink heavily, never drank alone, and his preference was for orderly gaiety. "I like to drink in company, have a good time, exchange opinions; there must be a point to drinking, like on a holiday, to keep up companionship." However, to his wife's chagrin, he did not shun the company of more disorderly drinkers.

A expressed his wishes and demands for support freely, with little embarrassment. His first response to the question about impossible things was that it would have been impossible for him as a young man to marry a beautiful heiress. When his wishes were frustrated he responded with anger rather than depression. He completed the sentence fragment "When he had nothing to eat. . ." with the words "he was angry", an unusual response. During the study he told both interviewers openly that he would like to have the interviewing extended for as many days as possible, so that he could earn more. When we had to refuse his request to guarantee him another full day's earnings, he did not show up the next day to complete the tests. Only once did A show some guilt feelings about his "oral demands"—in the context of discussing drinking as a factor in marital discord; but these feelings were not very pronounced.

A's strong wish for support did not make him a passive or dependent person; his passive attitudes were counterbalanced by his very considerable activity. His responses to the difficult situations in the Sentence Completions were about equally divided between the passive categories (discouragement, recourse to authorities or friends) and the self-assertive, active ones. The same situation obtained in the area of relationships to people, both fantasied and real: expressions of the wish to receive were counterbalanced by expressions of active concern for others. A early started supporting not only himself but also his family, accepting matter-of-factly the necessity of sharing his meager earnings; he gave up the flying training so as not to deprive his mother of his support; he tried to hasten his discharge from the sanitarium in order to start working and relieve his wife. In telling about his past he easily reproduced instances not only of friends helping him but also of his helping them, sometimes at some risk to himself. A's activity afforded him considerable pleasure; it did not seem to subserve any extraneous functions, such as fighting his "passive" wishes; the passive and the active trends, receiving and giving, existed side by side and both were accepted by him.

We have discussed various trends in A's strong drive for interaction with people: his wish for social harmony, for approval, for extending and sharing experience, for receiving and giving support and comfort. We have also seen that he was an active and vigorous person admiring determination in others and bent on carrying out his own plans. In general, all these trends were quite congruent; they included no wishes that threatened the social harmony A craved, such as wishes for domination or superiority over others. Still, in specific situations, with different partners, these various trends could get him into conflicts with others or with himself. To show how he solved such problems we shall review his relationships—and their antecedents—to his wife, to his equals (or people in general), and to authority.

f. Relation to Mother and to Wife

We start with A's relationship to his wife because he, himself, gave a large place to this topic and because the early relationship to his mother, reflected in the relationship to his wife, seemed to occupy a central place in his inner dynamics.

The fantasies produced by A on the TAT, taken in conjunction with his childhood memories, lead us to the following hypothetical reconstruction of his early significant experiences. A obtained a great deal of gratification from his mother, was "well nourished" by her; this early sound satisfaction formed a basis for his generally confident, optimistic outlook; as he said, he "took in strength" in childhood. Yet he had to share his busy hardworking mother with two brothers as well as with his father, and he must have experienced her periodical turning to others as "fickleness" threatening to deprive him of food as well as of love. These fantasies may have been supported by the reality of growing up in near-poverty, of the parents' constant concern with the success or failure of crops, and the father's stories of his own deprived childhood.

There was nothing in these early experiences that would interfere with the normal course of a boy's development; he took his father and his older brother as models and acquired a sound masculine identification without too much struggle and pain. Resentment of the rival was clear in A's relation to his older brother; how strong it was in relation to his father and to what extent it was repressed is not clear from the data. In the interviews he could not be induced to express any criticism of his father, but he gave the impression of conscious unwillingness rather than lack of awareness of parental shortcomings. What is clear from the evidence of projective techniques, is that the threat emanating from the father was fantasied in terms of control of means of sustenance, not in terms of physical punishment. This may help explain why A showed little evidence of any conflicts about aggression and about sex. The central theme of his fantasy was the relationship to his mother, the prototype of all life-sustaining gratifications, with its demands, quarrels, and reconciliations. The potency of this theme in his personality organization may be plausibly explained by the reinforcement of the early fantasies by later experiences; in his later childhood A went through a period of starvation which was followed by years of severe deprivation.

From A's report of his marriage it is clear that the feelings presumably originating in the early phases of his relation to his mother were quite alive in his relation to his wife. Yet the negative aspects of these feelings, the anger and jealousy produced by fantasies of deprivation, seemed to cause only minor disturbances; they did not prevent the marriage from being basically companionable and satisfying. In the TAT stories involving couples A typically discussed the situation from the point of view of each participant in turn, with a sympathetic understanding for their feelings. The "problematic" stories involved the woman's infidelity or the man's drinking; they usually ended in forgiveness and reconciliation, with both partners resuming responsible behavior. If they broke up, the man was confident of finding another woman, with whom he could have the good life he wanted. In his description of companionship in marriage, A stressed mutual understanding and support. He had this to say about the advantages of being married:

> "It is very bad to be all alone. Suppose I have finished my work and come home; what would I do next? Today I may have some interesting book and read a bit; or, say, you have to transcribe your stenographic notes; but once this is finished it isn't much fun to be alone. But if one is married, when the husband comes home they tell each other all things of interest that have happened, they talk

about housekeeping matters, make all sorts of plans for the future. . . .Even if things go badly, you share every-thing. . . .All of nature strives toward something, even animals, and no matter how you look at it, I think a per-son cannot suppress these strivings in himself, and the wish for married life is one of them. . . .Now, for instance, we are expecting our first child and I am very happy, no matter how difficult the circumstances. . . .I used to think at times: so you go on living and get to be forty—fifty years old; when you start declining in years, what interest will you have in life? But if you have a child, you are so glad and eager to get home; you want to play with him, see what he does, tell him stories. And I'll try to give him all the opportunities for education, let him choose the spe-cialty he wants, so he would never feel like reproaching me."

g. *Relation to Equals*

A had a remarkable ability to find solutions to interpersonal problems that both fulfilled the individual's wishes and pre-served social harmony. We shall illustrate his style of problem-solving by briefly reviewing his discussion of the issues posed in the Episodes, all of which he tackled very directly, without hesitation or doubts. His approach was based on the implicit assumption that people could always find a common ground if they would only understand each other's viewpoints and follow the general logic of human relationships. We shall give the gist of some of his proposed solutions, omitting the discussion of detail.

The overproducing worker (Episode 5) can be made to under-stand that his superior ability should not be misused to endanger other workers; but, if their poorer performance stems from un-willingness rather than inability, he has a good chance to con-vince them to work harder. In Episode 1, dealing with a child's refusal to go to school, the father and the teacher together can find the reasons behind his refusal; they must treat the child not according to some fixed rules, but in accord with his individual nature. In Episode 8, it is up to the foreman to find the real causes of the workers' decreasing output by inviting a frank discussion of their total situation, including their possible resentment of himself. The man rejected by his friends (Episode 6), when he finds out the reasons, can clear up the misunderstanding, or make amends if their complaint is justified. The friend who demands an undeserved recommendation (Episode 2) can be made to see the real reasons, including the other's concern for his own position, that make it impossible to grant his request, and can be offered help of a different kind. In Episode 4, the father will want to explain to the adult son why he would like him to take up a particular field of studies, but if the son does not come to see it his way, the father must realize that the choice is the son's, that he cannot live his life under coercion.

These solutions are not victories of one person over another; they are genuinely acceptable to both, regardless of their initial stands; they are the normative, the "ought" solutions. Such solutions are possible in reality only if the participants are capable of appreciating their logical validity; to put it differently, each must be willing to grant the "rightness" of the other's claim if he knows that he himself would make it in a similar situation. It is characteristic for A that in his formulations he did not overstress the normative character of these solutions; he assumed that most people would act in this reasonable way. The stories he told of his past suggest that he usually had no difficulty in following the reasonable course and expected others to follow it too. If they did not, he was not perturbed. He stood up for his rights when the situation called for it; if the other was stubbornly unreasonable he dissolved the relationship without much regret or rancor. His flexibility in adapting his actions to the turns of the situation was not hampered by excessive emotion; he showed little evidence of hostility or of strong fear. The following episode from A's past exemplifies his handling of "unreasonable" behavior in others. He told it in response to the question about his contacts with the Soviet authorities.

"I went to court once. I was still young then, and I went out in the street one night, playing the accordion (a highly valued, not easily replaceable possession). Then these two drunks came along and tried to take away my accordion. I resisted and told them they could dance to the music if they wanted to but had no right to break my instrument.

They beat me up and tore my clothes, and I brought them to court. Then their wives came, and all of them were afraid. They asked me to withdraw my complaint and offered to pay for the clothes. So they paid me, and then I said I didn't want to lodge a complaint, and that was all."

h. *Relation to Authority*

When unreasonable demands are made by superiors, open resistance may be futile and risky. In general A expected persons in authority to be human and reasonable like everybody else, and this expectation was founded on experience. His father meant well and was reasonable; so was his boss at the plant, who protected the workers' interests as much as he could. In most of the problematic situations of the Episodes A accorded no special treatment to the figures of authority. Yet, he had also experienced unjust and inhuman authority, although somewhat indirectly. Even if he, himself, had eventually been given a fair chance in the Soviet Union, he knew that his father's resistance to collectivization had brought him perilously close to losing this chance and had increased the danger of starvation for the family. In A's considered opinion, competence in work was the most important prerequisite for success in the Soviet Union, with Party membership and social origin in second and third place; but the dependence of survival on acceptance by the regime was also strong in his mind. An authority that had the power to feed or starve could not be approached without apprehension.

These doubts and misgivings were reflected in A's variable responses in projective techniques. He completed the sentence fragment "When the new director was appointed". . . in a hopeful spirit: the new director may put him in a better job. (It will be remembered that he considered the best jobs in the Soviet Union to be those in provisionment.) However, when his fantasy was stimulated by the visual images of the TAT his worries came to the fore. The picture of the store window evoked reflections about people who have no money and envy those who have; viewing pictures involving authority figures, he discussed their demands and threats, and possible bad consequences for the worker: "This demand of the foreman troubles the worker. Perhaps he has not fulfilled the norm; perhaps the foreman threatens to reduce his wages or even to fire him, you can figure it two ways." This "figuring it two ways" was also obvious when A, in viewing the picture of a meeting, misperceived one figure as Lenin and was unable to reconcile his presence with that of Stalin's portrait. As he associated Lenin with the plentiful NEP period and Stalin with famine and shortages, the image of authority was obviously not all of a piece in his mind. To deal with authority effectively and safely demanded care and thought.

A's proposed solution of the foreman-worker conflict about the best way of doing a piece of work (Episode 3) exemplifies his handling of unreasonable authority. "This is like with a German foreman: I tell him what way is best, but he keeps insisting. . . .Of course, if I have a reputation for good work, I can make my proposal, but if he refuses I would raise no fuss. And when he leaves I would do it my way, the better way. . . .I would do nothing to upset him and still do it my way. Of course, in most cases the worker will give in to the foreman." A's report of his work in the Soviet plant contained many examples of how he and his comrades found ways of circumventing the demands of authority. In discussing various aspects of Soviet life, he made matter-of-fact mentions of *blat,* Soviet slang term for illicit transactions of any kind based on personal connections or bribery.

 Thus, in strange contrast to his frankness and openness, A could be quite cunning in difficult situations and use concealment and deception in the service of self-preservation. The necessity of being on guard, of testing the new situations, imposed limits on his spontaneity and expressiveness and accounted for his controlled bearing. In spite of his strong wish for sociable sharing, he kept his own counsel when his best interest seemed to demand it. Without being actually suspicious he was guarded; his behavior during the study gave us many examples of this cautious approach. At first he concealed from us that he had been an officer in the Red Army, claiming the safer status of private; he came out with the truth only after several days of acquaintance. Similarly, he first told the interviewer he believed in God and later retracted this as untrue.

When asked to come for only a few more hours of testing, A handled this unwelcome request essentially as he had suggested the foreman in Episode 3 should be handled. He had hinted that the short time was not worth his while, but when the interviewer denied his request for a longer period, he neither refused to come nor showed any anger. Thus he avoided "upsetting" her at a time when he had not yet collected payment for services rendered. He simply didn't appear the next day, when his earnings could no longer be endangered by her displeasure. Intelligent, observant, and relatively well oriented, A also had the peasant's traditional slyness and was wary of situations he could not see through.

A does not seem to have had any guilt feelings about his readiness to deceive when expedient; he told of past deceptions frankly and did not feel compelled to justify them. This did not mean that he did not value honesty: he felt quite strongly about freedom to express one's true opinions and regretted the necessity to falsify them as "an insult to conscience and honor". Yet to A honesty was really vital only in friendships, in relationships of mutual trust. Where such a relationship was out of the question, violation of honesty did not upset him. He was ashamed if he failed to fulfill promises given to friends but saw no harm in cheating the authorities "when they asked for it".

The apprehensions about authority which underlay A's craftiness were well integrated by him and largely conscious. Quite conscious was their counterpart, namely his wish for an authority that would be generous in dispensing bounty, wise in teaching people to help themselves, and liberal in allowing free expression. In talking about his father A praised him both for insisting on education and for giving him some freedom of choice; this conception of parent-child relationship was reflected also in his conception of the ideal state. The government, he felt, should "guide the people" but it should also "listen to and obey the voice of the people". The state "must bring benefits to the people, so they will be happy. It should develop ideas and plans which will be useful for them, both for their daily needs and for their cultural life." In return "each citizen should have the sacred obligation to listen to the government and to obey its orders. If he does not understand them fully, the government should try to explain why something has to be done".

This description of the ideal state sounds like that of a kind and firm parent. Combining it with A's insistence on the equal value of all people and their right to speak their minds, we get the picture of a close happy family. A indeed wished for "the whole world being as one".

i. The Soviet State

In judging the state he knew, i.e., the Soviet Union, A was basically realistic; he accepted the communist ideals but was clearly aware of their failure, of the lack of freedom, the net of lies and pretenses created by the regime; his observations and judgments were free from distortion. Yet in his personal evaluation of the Soviet regime the positive aspects predominated over the negative ones, and he knew the reason; the state had enabled him to build a "good life" for himself, a better one than his father had had, a satisfying life in spite of all its limitations. Because of this, his criticism of the regime was not bitter, it was criticism by a family member who regretted the mistakes made by another and hoped he would mend his ways.

To maintain this hope A had to minimize in his own feelings the two severe blows the regime had dealt him: near-starvation early in life, and later his forced exile. When he was musing about the Soviet policies responsible for these blows, A came closest to rationalizations and excuses. Though he probably knew better, he half assumed, e.g., that any national government would consider a captured soldier a traitor; he wondered if Stalin's disregard for the material well-being of the population did not stem from his accurate estimate of how much hardship Russians were able to stand.

Along with wishfully trying to make his own state look better than it was, A may have projected some of his suppressed anger into the image of the foreign attacker. Before war broke out he felt troubled and full of anger when he read in the papers about the foreign countries' preparations for war and thought of the Russian youth who would fall on the battlefield. When war became a reality, he killed Germans beyond the call of duty, as a sniper, in revenge for his brother's death. But if the emotions naturally aroused in A by his loss and by the invasion of his country were intensified by some emotions stemming from other sources, this displacement remained reversible; it did not result in fixed or stereotyped attitudes. After telling about his sniper activities, he expressed some guilt; these particular Germans may not have been guilty of atrocities, he said, but one could not help feeling hatred after seeing the countryside ravaged. Similarly, his hopes for the Soviet regime's improvement did not lead him to justify its misdeeds or to nurture wishful expectations. A's realism is best shown by the fact that, once taken prisoner, he never gave credence either to the rumors of radical changes in the Soviet Union, or to assurances of clemency for the returnees; he was never tempted to return.

D. Awareness and Conflict

A did not seem to have any elaborate or rigid defenses against his feelings and impulses; they were successfully held in check by realistic considerations, by conscious caution. This left him considerable freedom of expression in safe situations. We have seen that in the projective techniques he gave free rein to his fantasy and derived pleasure from expressing some of his wishes in extreme ways. Yet hardly a single trend appeared in these fantasies that did not figure also in his reality-oriented discussions. In describing his various trends in this essay, we were able to draw examples from his descriptions of his past and present life, his projective tests, his expressions of sentiments and opinions; we did not have to distinguish between the data from various levels because they were so strongly congruent. This is equivalent to saying that A's impulses and emotions were present in his awareness, even if in a non-reflective way. He was, in fact, in close touch with most of them and accepted them easily. Not sensing within himself any wishes he could not accept, A did not know what it meant to feel divided against himself. This was strikingly shown when the interviewer repeatedly asked him the projective questions about the *wishes* he found *hard to suppress,* rejecting his initial attempt to list instead the situations he found hard to bear. Faced with this suggestion of an *inner* conflict, A said with real astonishment: "But who could force any wishes on me?" He rejected steadfastly all the examples of possibly objectionable wishes the interviewer supplied him with, substituting examples of wishes frustrated by the reality situation alone; he concluded by saying that when he had a very strong wish he was sure to make it come true sooner or later. Either A had repressed nothing, or else he had repressed some impulses so successfully that they led to no disturbances and conflicts.

There is one exception to this statement. Among the many themes which A brought up with some frequency there was one—and only one—which he did not handle alike in his fantasy and in his explicit discussion and judgment: the theme of betrayal. Like his comrades, A had despised all those who denounced others and had steered clear of them. This issue was obviously important to him; he reacted very strongly when he was wrongly accused of being an informer. However, in fantasy A occasionally identified with persons who really had betrayed their friends and were accused or persecuted by them. To the projective question about possible causes of insanity, A replied: "When someone is being persecuted, perhaps he has indeed done something that is bad for the people, and now his friends tell him frankly that he has done a bad thing, for instance denounced somebody. He starts thinking about what he has done, all the consequences of it, and he may lose his mind."

When his older brother joined the Secret Police, A may have worried about his friends' reactions to this event, or he may have tried to conceal it from them; his preoccupation with the issue of informing may have stemmed from that. Yet it is also possible that A himself was more tempted to follow in his brother's footsteps than he realized. Perhaps at some time he had fantasies of ingratiating himself with the regime by denouncing friends and thus insuring a bountiful life for himself, and this had kept the themes of betrayal and guilt alive in his mind. This possibility is suggested by some of the sentence completions. A completed the fragment: "When his subordinates disobeyed"... by the words: "he was obliged to report it". Still more striking is his "keep *me* under watch", to the fragment "Andrew's co-workers". This completion is both unusual in general and atypical for A.

In real life, when dealing with a suppressive authority A

would try to cheat it; if cunning did not work he would simply submit to it. In fantasy, however, he may have visualized placating and bribing it by denouncing others. This method may have been foreshadowed in his childhood dealings with his parents and brothers and in fantasies of how he could win in the scramble for scarce supplies; such fantasies could easily become the focus of an unconscious conflict. Because of A's great dependence on harmonious relationships with friends, a temptation for such course of action would be more disturbing to him than the fantasies that underlay the quarrels and reconciliations with his wife; he would never have thought of the latter as possibly leading to insanity.

If A did have a conflict centered on the theme of betrayal, then his lack of awareness of the personal reference of this theme was his Achilles' heel, the only weak spot in his sound and sturdy organization. One might speculate about the kinds of pressures that could cause this organization to break down and to lose out to the neurotic system which (so far) existed merely as a potentiality. Such breakdown and reversal could be brought about by a situation in which, in A's perception, the only way to insure survival for himself and his family would be to betray his friends. Once he had committed such an act, he would have been unable to preserve his wholeheartedness; divided against himself, he would have had to start building a protective system of tenuous assumptions to deny or to justify the breach between his beliefs and his actions. Fortunately, a person as competent as A is not likely to find himself in such an extreme situation, no matter how unfavorable the circumstances. When, in his native country, people were being pressed into the service of the secret police he was not faced with this choice: as a skilled worker, he had an alternative road to survival and success. We shall conclude by quoting from an earlier essay on a similar case by one of the authors. The quote applies equally well to A.

"Central to his adjustment was the possession of technical skills that were highly needed and valued. These skills insured him higher material rewards and a more considerate treatment than are granted by the regime to the more easily replaceable labor force of peasants and unskilled workers who can be dealt with summarily. Skilled work was also a source of inner satisfaction for Boris, and part of a basis for his self-respect. On the other hand, he shared with the less skilled manual workers the external and internal advantages presented by the relatively low position in the social hierarchy, and by the irrelevance to his job of all ideological issues. These advantages are the relative immunity from the grave risks with which all administrative responsibilities are fraught in the Soviet Union, and a relative freedom from pressures for ideological conformity, for the 'double think' which is involved in following the changing Party line, but which does not work in dealing with the machines. From what we know about the workings of the Soviet social system, the position of a skilled worker, of a low grade manual technician, which combines the advantages of a minimum 'specialist status' with a relative freedom from ideological pressures and decisions, is the one that presents the best opportunities for the adjustment of the kind achieved by Boris. People in this position have a chance to obtain substantial, if limited satisfactions without sacrificing their inner integrity, a possibility not equally available to those in other positions" (2).

Chapter 3

VLADIMIR—A YOUNG COMMUNIST

A. *Behavior in the Interview*

Vladimir, a twenty-nine-year-old unmarried graduate of a military academy, born in 1921, fought in the war as a Red Army officer and was taken prisoner by the Germans during their advance into Russia. An active member of the Communist Youth Organization (Komsomol) since adolescence, he was by that time somewhat disillusioned in Stalin's regime and vaguely hoped for major changes after the war. In the prisoners' camps he nearly died of starvation. Later he found his way into the German-sponsored Russian Army of Liberation, where he first worked as a propagandist and then as a personal guard of the leader, General Vlasov. As for all Vlasovites, the early postwar years were full of dangers for V; he barely escaped being lynched by a mob, was hunted by the Soviet Repatriation Commission, and spent some time in hiding. After his status had been legalized by the Allies, V chose not to live in a camp and supported himself by journalism, by working as a draftsman and sometimes as a laborer. Because of his communist and Vlasovite past, V's chances for being admitted to the United States were poor, and he, himself, was not eager to emigrate; he felt this would mean a final break with his country. He thought a war with Russia was imminent and felt that, if well conducted by the Allies, it could mobilize the popular discontent and bring about the fall of the Soviet regime. He wished to take part in the struggle, hoping against hope that he might return to his country as a liberator and participant in the work of reform.

Of average height, sturdy, neatly dressed, V was calm and slightly reserved in the interview, which he viewed as serving our common cause. He usually waited for questions and then answered them readily and fully, talking in a low voice but expres-

85

sively. He described all events, including the most harrowing
ones, objectively and analytically, yet vividly; his description
of the psychosis of starvation, e.g., included a wealth of observations, both introspective and objective. He discussed personal
topics without hesitation and with obvious sincerity, but he did
not actively promote personal interaction with the interviewer;
she felt less immediate emotional contact with him than with
most of the other Russian subjects.

V's equanimity and control became somewhat strained when
he worked on projective tests, and this tension found partial
release in jokes. He said with some embarrassment, that he felt
like a guinea pig and that it made him uncomfortable to be
"pried into", but that it was his duty to cooperate. He regained
control by asking intelligent questions about the rationale of
the tests, and tried to reestablish harmony by assuring the interviewer that the experience was profitable to him: similar methods
and tests might be used in the Russia of tomorrow. He was
genuinely pleased with her commenting on the originality of
some of his test responses.

B. Life History, Personal and Political

a. Childhood and Parents

Born in Central Russia, V was the third and youngest son of a
middle peasant who, upon returning from the First World War,
worked as a lumberjack while his wife worked their land. During the period of the New Economic Policy (NEP), when private
initiative was encouraged by the government, the father built up
a small enterprise, a cobbler's shop, employing apprentices
along with his elder sons. This was the affluent period for the
family. Before the government's policy was reversed, V's father
read the signs of things to come. He closed his shop and returned
to the "semi-proletarian" status of lumber worker long before
collectivization of farming reached his village; he was among the
first peasants to join the kolkhoz. V was nine years old when
this change for the worse took place. Lean years began for the
collectivized village. The situation improved only slightly and
gradually up to the outbreak of the war. V was undernourished
and poorly clad, especially during the years of secondary school

when he lived by himself in a nearby town; but no hardships seemed too great when the goal was education.

Early in his school years V joined the Pioneers; at first he merely enjoyed the organized games, but gradually he acquired some political concepts. "I knew that a capitalist is a man with a big belly and a cigar who burns coffee to increase his profits while the workers starve. A kulak is a man who exploits the peasants. Wreckers are educated people who don't care about the nation's wealth and indulge in sabotage." Like his brothers, a Party and Komsomol man, respectively, V stood up for the regime when his parents cursed it, but later he was caught up in the anti-Soviet sentiments that were surging all around him. His brother spoke against forced collectivization at a Komsomol meeting and was temporarily expelled. V himself had a chance to talk with the convicts employed in construction work near his village; he discovered that these "enemies of the people" were no poster-kulaks but the same kind of peasants as his own family and friends. For a while, V counted himself in the opposition; he wrote anti-Soviet poetry, repeated anti-Soviet jokes, and drew caricatures of Stalin, until his brother told him to be more cautious and not to endanger their parents. At the age of fourteen he made friends with a young worker who gave him Party literature and explained the regime's stern policies by likening the Party to a strict father who must impose temporary privations and punishments on his children for the sake of building a new house. This explanation and the friend's sincere belief helped resolve V's early doubts. He became a convinced communist and at sixteen joined the Komsomol with very high expectations. He wanted to be a builder of communism, to belong to a strong organized group, and in due time to pass from the Communist Youth Organization to Party membership proper. V's plans created no problems in the family. The parents realized that their sons must accept the new framework of life if they were to achieve a higher social status. Family solidarity was enhanced, not threatened, by this step. V himself, however, unlike some of his contemporaries, viewed his joining the Komsomol not as an expediency measure but as a personal commitment to a high goal and a vital life task.

Before following the political vicissitudes of V's adolescence, we shall take a look at his childhood, the prepolitical stage of his life. He was born to middle-aged parents, the junior of his brothers by eight and thirteen years. A sickly child who went through numerous illnesses, he was sensitive, was apt to cry when frustrated, and harbored many intense fears: of darkness, fire, water, crowds. During the first four years of his life, when his father worked away from the village and his mother was busy farming, he was looked after by his brothers or by the grandmother who lived nearby. Yet his father's visits were among V's very first memories; father brought presents and told fascinating stories about his life as a soldier, about the army and war. He fulfilled V's ardent wish by giving him a rifle before he was four years old. V furiously defended his weapon when neighbors teasingly pretended to take it away from him; he had already absorbed the idea that a soldier does not hand over his arms. He daydreamed of going to war together with his father and worried about whether he would be taken along. The father was clearly the hero of V's early childhood.

From his present perspective V saw an important flaw in his father's character; an attitude of superiority, a compelling wish to rise above other peasants. He explained it by his father's past. A self-made man who had early left home to escape his own tyrannical father, he had gone through a period of drinking and drifting before settling down. He liked to display the material success he had temporarily achieved, sought the company of the village intelligentsia, and wanted his sons to surpass their friends and rise in the world: "We were always told—don't be like the rest." The father had particularly high expectations for V, to whom he was able to give material and educational advantages— toys, books—during his childhood, and whom he later supported through high school, regardless of the sacrifices involved. The goal was professional status which the older brothers were unable to achieve because they had to go to work early: "My father said in front of everybody that he would make me an educated man." The choice of future profession was left to V, but his father used every opportunity to make the child want to learn. The high-status visitors—the teachers, the priest—would show up his ignorance by catching him in error or asking puzzling questions. In the interview V expressed appreciation of his father's efforts to fire his ambition, and denied any connection with his own conflicts about superiority. Yet he was left with a strong feeling that the father gave him an education largely because of his own vanity: "for the sake of knowing that *he* had made us equal to anyone: *my* sons!"

All in all, V had kept a predominantly positive image of his father; he saw him as strong, competent, self-possessed, and as kind and generous to inferiors. He praised him as a good educator who showed no favoritism, used no physical punishment, and even abstained from swearing, scolding, and lecturing; he would merely tell the son to think it over whether what he had done was good or bad. When the teacher asked him to put a stop to V's misdeeds (such as carrying a weapon or reading *The Count of Monte Cristo* in school), he would reply that he had no control over his child, that the school was in charge; this was a self-protective device commonly used by the peasants. The father impressed on his sons that they must handle themselves so as not to expose the parents to shame or danger. This, together with the value of education for rising in the world, and with heroic traditions of military service, seems to have been the father's message to V. Except in his early years, he never felt close to his father, though he kept his respect and liking for him. The middle brother, who used to tease V in his childhood, later became his ideal; he felt free to share with this brother some of his problems and perplexities.

V described his mother as a persistent, careful, hardworking woman who supported her husband's decisions but was also a respected member of the village community in her own right; she learned to read and write during the campaign against illiteracy, when she was fifty years old. She did not figure very prominently in V's early memories, but we did get a glimpse of their interactions. At the age of four V spent two months with his mother in Moscow, receiving treatment for the bite of a mad dog; fascinated and frightened by the many new impressions, he was at first afraid of the hospital. His mother overcame his resistance to treatment by ingenious enticements, but she also exploited his fears. When a patient was wheeled by with his tongue hanging out and his eyes bulging, she told V that the same would happen to him if he persisted in refusing treatment.

Other frightening scenes, such as the militia chasing after people, she explained in a similar fashion: "they did not do as they should, like you when you did not want to go to the hospital". Unlike the father, the mother was religious, and so the ikons remained in the house. The son received no religious instruction and, in line with his evolving communist beliefs, considered himself an atheist; yet he attended church services, because he enjoyed the singing and the beauty of the ritual.

When V was six years old his father took to drink, and the next two years were the worst in the child's life. The mother was often able to soothe the father, but the boys had to leave the house when he was drunk: "He would not knowingly harm us, but he drank so much that he saw things and might mistake one of us for a thief." V explained his father's drinking bouts by his relative idleness at the time of the cobbler's shop; the drinking stopped when he returned to lumber work. The chronology of events makes it more likely that the father started drinking when he realized that his modest material success would not be allowed to continue.

V's eighth year, when he entered school, marked a turn toward greater well-being and greater activity. This may have been due to his improved health or to the change in the family constellation: with the shop closed the father was once more an infrequent visitor at home, and both brothers had left the village. Vladimir had early learned to read and write and school was easy for him. He had also become an imaginative and forceful leader in the games of the village children, and their exploits continued in school. His happiest memories of these years were of running away when kept after school for punishment ("to run away was a feather in your cap") and of participating in intergroup fighting: "I tried to be out in front, even though I was the smallest." He worked at overcoming his fears; instead of hiding under the bed when there was a fire, he now joined the fire brigade. He cultivated the company of older boys and tried to follow their lead in every way. They made him climb the bell tower, walk through the cemetery at night; "I was scared but I knew I had to do it, or I would lose their company forever." When at sixteen V was accepted into the Komsomol he had a reputation for ability, courage, and leadership.

b. Adolescence

Initially his high expectations were fulfilled. A close group quickly formed among the new Komsomol members; they shared activities, daydreams, and thoughts. V was elected to various posts, was a Pioneer leader, acquired experience in organizational work, and gained in scope and stature. In villages he and his friends would receive the peasants' complaints and pass them on to the agencies in town; they felt needed and recognized. The pressure from above at this period was moderate, the guidance was not over-strict. The young people felt free to ask questions of their Party member leaders. Even though they had to carry out orders they were not afraid to criticize and object. They could also be lighthearted and gay, and life was exciting and romantic.

This happy situation lasted less than two years, until the general purge spread to the Komsomol. In the course of the next two years the members of V's group, including himself, were led to denounce one another, often unwittingly or in self-protection, as disloyal or deviationist. His girl friend, whose family was suspect, had to leave town, and to correspond with her was reprehensible. The spirit of mutual trust and of devotion to the cause was destroyed. V himself survived the purge and retained his membership, although he was repeatedly censured and removed from his posts, but his wholehearted belief in the Party was gone. "It was like being a split personality; externally we kept on working, but internally we did not care any more." He came close to repudiating Stalin's regime as an egoistically motivated distortion of Lenin's goals, leading to terror and slavery. When in later years he was urged to join the Party, he refused, giving the acceptable reason that he was not yet mature enough to be worthy of membership. Yet he continued to be active in the Komsomol, in spite of his feeling that it had become a mere appendage of the Party. The youth organization had no part in setting up the regime's policies which he rejected, and it still offered some of the satisfactions he craved; to resign from it would have meant utter isolation.

During the last year of high school, when the worst upsets in the Komsomol were over, V lived through a major personal crisis; the disillusioning experiences were brought to bear on the

decisions he had to make about his future. Influenced by books
and films, he had wanted to become a geologist, a profession
combining adventure, discovery, enjoyment of nature, and
valuable service to the state. Now he felt discouraged from this
plan, as in fact from any professional work. "I had felt all the
blows of Soviet life; I knew they would continue, whether I was
a geologist or an engineer; getting an education was of no use.
In those conditions I could not act normally, I could not be
useful. Only people who can lie and pretend can work in this
atmosphere safely; my thoughts would come into the open
sooner or later." V's solution was to follow the example of his
brother and to enter a military school, though this meant giving
up the goal set for him by his father of becoming a highly-edu-
cated professional man. The army looked like a refuge from
political involvements, yet offering a chance of leadership, service, and prestige. "I thought that in the army you march left,
you march right, and that's all, there are no politics." This was
also a decision in favor of material security: in the military
school, for the first time since his childhood, V was well fed,
well clad, and had some money to spend. The decision in fact
proved a wise one; after overcoming the initial shock of subjection to strict discipline, V oriented and organized himself
so as to avoid all but minor collisions with the authorities. He
formulated for himself the principle of "inner emigration":
"I could follow the service life and yet live my inner life which
was of no concern to anyone." He excelled in his studies and
received a better general education that he had expected; when
war broke out he was an officer, and thus in a better position
than his university friends who were drafted as privates.
   Practical considerations, however, do not adequately explain
V's decision to give up his professional aspirations. He had lost
confidence in himself: "I realized that I would not be a good
geologist, that in general I was good for nothing. So I got the
idea that I would defend the safety of those who were more
gifted than I; it was an act of sacrifice on my part." Although
V's school studies had suffered during the upsets in the Komsomol, he had no realistic reasons for doubting his superior
ability. He had good reasons, however, for doubting the prospects of success, his chances of attaining and keeping a position

of leadership. He had blamed Stalin, the perverter of Lenin's ideals, for the injustices he had suffered at the hands of the Party, but these thoughts lacked clarity and conviction. Emotionally he took the blame on himself; it was not merely an excuse when he warded off Party membership by pleading incomplete understanding. The inner crisis continued even after the practical decisions had been made. During his first year at the academy V was plagued by a sense of futility and questioned the meaning of life. The dialectic materialism he was studying only contributed to his dejection since it stressed the unimportance of the individual, his inability to influence the course of historic events. He found no solutions, but in time his despondency wore off, the sickness passed, life reasserted itself: "I found only this answer: since you are alive you've got to live on." This unresolved crisis was probably crucial in shaping V's private view of the world, a view which was little affected by further changes in his political opinions and allegiances.

c. Disaffection

V's belief in the power of the Soviet state was undermined by the course of the Finnish war and by the initial disorganization produced by the German attack. His personal bitterness flared up when, having been left behind, wounded, in a town taken by the Germans, he painfully made his way to the Russian side, only to be accused of treason and threatened with execution. He was saved by the intercession of a friend high up in the army. But the worst blow of all was the discovery that it was the Germans, not the Red Army, whom the Russian peasant welcomed as liberators. He swore that after the war there would be a reckoning with the oppressors who had alienated the people. Still, he not only fought loyally, but also fully accepted the dictum that it was shameful and treasonable to save one's life by surrendering. "When I was taken prisoner, I inwardly condemned myself, I knew I was an outlaw." Ill with typhus, V fainted at the very moment of capture and thus escaped having to choose between suicide and surrender. When he was later forced to interpret for the Germans he tried to use the situation for propaganda against them and for estab-

lishing contact with the Soviet partisans. It was not until he had
had many contacts with Russian intellectuals that V revised his
political conceptions, making totalitarianism, instead of Stalin,
responsible for oppression and terror. This change enabled him
to join Vlasov's army and, after the Allied victory, to pin his
hopes for radical changes in Russia on the combined effects of
foreign war and popular uprising.

The political system V now favored did not differ much from
that outlined by most other DPs; it combined all the features of
a social welfare state and partial state control of production
with maximum freedom for the individual. He felt confident
that the peasants, once the land was restored to them, would
start forming partial collectives of their own free will. He favored
trial by jury for all Party members; each should account for his
own course and be judged on his own merits; he expected that
only a minority would be found guilty of crimes against the
people.

C. Basic Ideology

A portrait of V as a person can perhaps best be drawn by elucidating his view of the nature of human existence. This area of
"basic ideology" was the one in which, in the interviews, he
showed the greatest involvement and made most insightful self-
descriptive comments.

According to V, the basic datum of human existence is the
person in society (in the "collective"), and the person's basic
problem, his life task, is to evolve ways to be fully one's individual self and yet fully a member of the community. The two
parts of this task are equally important, neither must be sacrificed to the other, and only their harmonious synthesis makes
the person whole and genuine. "A human being cannot be genuine if he lets his behavior be determined by the dictates of

society; a person must act from within, as he truly is—not lead
a double existence; and only that person is really good whose
inner life naturally coincides with social ethics." It was V's
professed belief that such harmony is possible, that in fact a
person is most valuable for another and for the group if he has
fully developed his unique individual assets and uses them to
produce socially valuable results; each individual does have

something unique, each one is valuable, and—contrary to the Marxist dogma— each one can, within limits, influence the course of major events if he has developed his willpower and personal strength. No individual can have absolute freedom; one person's freedom collides with that of another, and the conflict must be solved by mutual concessions, often with unavoidable pain. Yet this necessity for self-limitation is amply compensated for by being valuable to others and valued by them; participation in a larger social whole, service to a cause, give meaning to a person's life. To isolate oneself from the whole, to betray it, is to destroy this meaning and to betray oneself. Self-isolation is the root of all evil, the cardinal sin.

These formulations had been thought through and felt through; they are admirable in their force and clarity and have a strong kinship with the thinking of the holistic personality theorists (Adler, Goldstein, Maslow, Angyal) who view self-actualization and social feeling, or self-assertion and surrender, as the two basic and complexly interwoven human trends. To what extent and in what ways had V himself been able to pursue these two directions and to resolve the conflicts inherent in this duality? He conceived of the ideal person as one who has will-power, originality, and integrity; who is genuine and sincere, self-reliant, slave neither to public opinion nor to his own passions, ready and willing to stand up for himself, yet also capable of effective social action. When asked about his main source of satisfaction in life, V replied without hesitation: "People; I want to understand a man, to find a common language, to influence him." His concept of friendship implied mutual appreciation and loyalty, some readiness for sacrifice and for yielding: "I need not rule over my friend." He preferred to have one close friend and a wide range of acquaintances; he expected to find some good in the worst and some flaws in the best; inconsistencies, reversals of attitudes never surprised him.

These formulations represent V's blueprint for effectively combining self-realization and service. We must now consider how he, himself, fared on all these scores: how "strong" a person he actually was and felt himself to be, how close he was to people, and what kind of satisfactions he sought and obtained from them.

D. *Personality*

a. *Concordant Attitudes*

V's self-description as active, determined, self-reliant is borne out by the way he had handled many difficult situations in his past when survival depended on resourcefulness. He had also repeatedly stood up for his rights and for those of others, directly when feasible, with cunning when necessary, often taking personal risks for the sake of his plans or his comrades. In the point of "control of passions" V did not fully live up to his ideal of strength; though he usually acted with forethought, he lost his temper at times, or gave in to temptation and forgot caution, e.g., drank in the company of people whom he did not know well. On the whole, however, he was satisfied with the measure of self-control he possessed; he did not seem to have much conflict about aggression and about sex and did not over-stress control of these impulses. Some episodic conflicts in these areas had been resolved by him not in terms of "control of passions" but in terms of the interpersonal issues involved.

V's experiences taught him caution; his discussions of how to protect one's safety in the Soviet Union were detailed and realistic. He had not become indiscriminately suspicious, even after living through the postwar persecution of Vlasovites. He had never been an isolate, either within or outside Russia, but had safely made some close friends, even in the groups that he knew contained many informers. He was free from racial and other prejudices and no groups were used by him as scapegoats. He was not overawed by the authorities and responded differently to good and bad superiors. In his dealings with friends and companions V usually lived up to his standards of frankness; he could, in fact, be quite blunt. In dealing with interpersonal situations in the Episodes Test he stressed honesty (within limits dictated by caution), reasonable self-assertion, rational discussion, and mutual adaptation. His discussion revealed some interpersonal difficulties, but no marked fears or serious conflicts. V was not unaware of the difficulties. He realized, e.g., that his own competitive feelings sometimes made it difficult for him to be fair and objective: "When I want *my* project to be accepted, it is hard for me to see the advantage of any

conflict — wanted to be individual

other." Yet under favorable conditions, as in his first Komsomol group, V's pleasure in cooperation greatly outweighed the pain of any frictions arising in his interaction with others.

b. Discordant Attitudes

1. Unresolved Contradictions

V spoke with nostalgia of the all-too-brief happy period of his youth; though he had never been inactive and alone, his satisfactions in life had obviously fallen short of his wishes. His image of himself as strong and competent, unified within himself and able to withstand pressure, was belied by the evidence of his fantasies and, in part, by his conscious self-perception. The contradictions in his comments indicate unresolved conflicts. Let us look at some of these contradictions.

V believed that a strong tie to the group, the "collective", was central to the Russian character and Russian tradition; he assigned to Western culture individualism and narrow self-interest; Russian literature, he stressed, contained no idealized "lone wolves", such as Jack London's heroes. Yet he was obviously fascinated with the romantic image of one who is "different", exceptional, enigmatic. He talked about the strong support a person receives from the group, and told of inmates of a Soviet prison who joined a hunger strike declared by one of them for personal reasons; he quoted the Russian proverb: "In company death itself is sweet." Yet he, himself, had avoided moving into a DP camp because he feared for his inner integrity: "The camp atmosphere sucks you in and makes you change; the herd instinct develops, your interests become petty." He also had some fear of groups on a physical level. As a child he was afraid of being caught in a melee, and the most frightening thing he could think of now was a hostile mob. V's wish for independence sometimes led to behavior that was almost bizarre. When looking up a person in a strange town, he would not ask for directions nor consult a map; he liked to find the street on his own, by "intuition", regardless of wasted time. Hand in hand with the fear of being influenced and changed by the group, of being or becoming a mere "grain of sand", went the fear of losing the group's support, of which more later.

The fear of being weak, lost, insignificant, was the negative counterpart of V's activity and independence. However, his self-image also included more positive aspects which might have functioned as complements of the "strong" self if fully accepted by him. Emotional sensitivity, tenderness, esthetic enjoyment were not entirely suppressed or rejected, but neither were they completely integrated with his self-image. He partly accepted these moods and qualities under the category of "intuition", a special possession which made him interesting and "different"; yet he also felt that they were inconsistent with his manly posture and made him a split, problematic person. When, in responding to the blank TAT card, V had a chance to give his fantasy free reins, he visualized a "darkened, tastefully furnished room" with a lamp illuminating a vase of flowers and a gun. These, he said, showed a rift in the inhabitant's mind: "He cannot always be looking at flowers, he must also fight for his life." The theme of inner duality was clearly expressed in V's report of an episode involving his girl friend, which occurred after a long separation, on the eve of his leaving for the front. After a day of heavy drinking with his comrades, he had made some sexual advances to the girl. She later scolded him for his impulsive behavior and his subsequent halfhearted apologies. V replied, in writing: "Two friends of mine are here: one is X (his school nickname) who was so upset by your letter that he wrote two answers and tore them up; and now it is me, Lieutenant Y, who has this to say to you: if you really love me, love me the way I am, with my good qualities and my defects; what kind of love would it be otherwise?" The girl answered that the lieutenant was the one who understood her, even if the other was close to her heart, and that she had decided to follow him to the front as a nurse.

2. *Self-Image as Artist*

V's ideal of aggressive manliness prevented him from fully accepting his own capacity for sensitive empathic perception of his surroundings. Yet he highly valued art, a product of that soil. One of his favorite fantasied roles was that of "creative artist", and the fantasy had some basis in reality. V not only enjoyed art and literature but had some literary aspirations of his own. He let the interviewer read his first attempt, a well-written autobiography. He would like, he said, to write a novel about a young communist changing into a dedicated fighter against communism, but for such a novel to be more than a personal document more erudition and creative fantasy was required than he possessed: "My pride, or my vanity, does not permit me to write unless I know I *can* write." In the TAT V told a number of stories dealing with the creative artist's fate; these stories throw light on the issue that was personally important for him.

The artist in these stories did not fare too well. The talented hero of the first story (Card 1), though his dream of becoming a musician comes true, is still an unhappy man, because "artists as a rule are misfits, they live in a different world; in real life they are not successful". In another story (Card 4) a painter seeking new ways in art lives in poverty, unable to sell his pictures; he is provoked to violent anger by the slighting remarks of an ignoramus. But his wife stands by him and, after ups and downs, he may be able to find a place in society. In the story about Card 5, an art student discovers that his landlady shares his esthetic tastes; this "makes him realize that a human being similar to him is living beside him". A romance develops and they are happy, but "who knows for how long". In still another story (Card 18) an actor absorbed in reliving his first successful performance is brought down to earth by a robber's attack.

This series of stories suggests that V's professed belief in a harmonious synthesis of creative self-expression and social participation was counterbalanced by doubt. He feared that isolation was the price of originality, either because the creative individual is asocial or because the milieu is indifferent or hostile.

c. Social Leadership

In his actual work in the Komsomol and the army V had to deal with people and exercise leadership; the problem of how to be a creative social leader was of greater importance for him than the problems facing the artist. One spectacular aspect of the leadership role attracted him greatly: heroic sacrificial action in the service of the group or the cause; this had been

one of the lures of the military career. Though V later dismissed
his wish for a heroic role as youthfully romantic, the theme
was reflected in some of his answers to Projective Questions.
He told of how reluctant he had been to send a subordinate on
a dangerous mission if he had not exposed himself to the same
danger first. If he had only six months to live he would like to
return to Russia, talk with all his friends, and then "commit a
central terroristic act", such as killing Stalin. In reality V repeatedly took serious risks in order to help others. When he
once successfully crossed a border while his inexperienced
companion was caught, he returned to share his friend's fate;
this act gave him great satisfaction. Heroism was one solution to
V's dilemma of serving others while also satisfying his strong
wish "to act differently from everybody else, or from the majority, and to be widely known".

Such a wish is not easily fulfilled in everyday work situations,
where it may interfere with effective social functioning. V was
not unaware of this danger: "I must always consider the interests of others, I don't want to infringe on them, yet the wish is
there." But his awareness did not extend to all aspects of the
situation. Having resolved on the ideological level the dilemma
of the individual's powerlessness, he failed to see that the
strength of his wish to be noticed, to be strong and effective,
derived from his feeling of personal insignificance. Correspondingly, he was not aware of how often his desire to display his
"difference" and to have an impact blinded him to others'
needs, so that an action which was meant to lead and serve
them was perverted into covert domination. He recalled the
periodic revolts of his childhood playmates against his leadership but ascribed these revolts largely to their envy of his superiority. He gave strikingly frank descriptions of how he disliked
to see his friends get out from under his influence; of how he
laid careful plans to "take them in hand" again; he told of
getting irritated and losing his temper when someone's mal-
performance or negligence threatened his control of the situation; but he justified his reactions, in part, by pointing to the
generally deleterious results of upsetting plans once made. He
described anger and withdrawal, or at least a temptation to
withdraw, as his alternative reactions to loss of control over

others. Yet, in another context, he explained the "strange contrast" of his quick temper and coldness by the Ugro-Finnish blood of his ancestors, no longer viewing his moods as personal responses to frustration. It would seem that V was only partly aware of the strength of his power orientation, which was ideologically unacceptable to him. Nevertheless, he handled the resulting difficulties quite effectively by maintaining intellectual control over situations and deliberate control over his actions.

In some situations such strict control was not needed. V repeatedly spoke of an experience which had given him deep joy—his success as a Pioneer leader in reforming a near-delinquent nine-year-old boy of whom everyone else had despaired. By careful observation he discovered the boy's "weak spot"— his hidden aspiration to a "heroic" soldierly role. He encouraged this aspiration and made the boy his assistant. In telling the story he stressed that his trust had been sincere and that the boy had known it. This approach eventually resulted in an enduring change in the boy; V earned his devotion and his family's gratitude. In this instance his ingenious educational action met the other's need and resulted in interpersonal harmony. The importance of this episode for V may have been reinforced by memories of his own childhood. When his father gave him a gun he had not been sure whether this present of a real weapon was only a joke or whether his father truly accepted him as a soldierly companion, a rightful bearer of a gun. In reenacting the episode in a parental role he gave it a happy ending.

d. The Meaning of the "Collective"

So far we have discussed V's social relationships in face-to-face groups. His relation to the "collective" in its supra-individual meaning—as an organization, a nation, a common cause—is best elucidated by his reaction to having been separated both from his country and from any strong organized group. Some aspects of this reaction are projected into the story about the TAT card which shows a boy huddled on the floor (Card 3).

"This young woman worked as an intelligence agent during the war; she carried out many important missions.

This work was her life; she had not been forced, she did not do it for money, nor just for adventure; it was her sport, but she also acted on her ideological convictions. The war ended with her country's defeat, she barely managed to avoid jail. She had not achieved her goal, all her hopes had failed, the country was in a chaos; she managed to live somehow, miserably. She must find a way out, but she had no strength left. In a moment of despair she took the gun she had hidden away, she decided to commit suicide. Half an hour of thinking, and the gun fell from her hand, she wasn't strong enough to carry out her intention; she has dropped to the floor, despondent, but she isn't going to put the gun to her temple again. This is the turning point in her life. She will become an ordinary woman, wear a dress, get a typist's job, and only secretly hope for the time when her work may be needed once more."

In the story about a dimly illumined figure at night (Card 20), V vividly depicted the loneliness of a man in a strange country: he has acquaintances, but his close friends are far away and he spends his evenings in solitary walks, reliving his past and dreaming of returning home.

There is little doubt that feelings of resignation and depression formed the constant background of V's life in exile. To counteract them he had to cling to the belief in imminent changes which would enable him to return home as a liberator and reformer; he took an active part in the émigrés' political activities in order to prepare himself for this role. The unsettled situation of the time lent some plausibility to these hopes, but not enough to provide a basis for realistic personal plans. Not many other young DPs refrained, as V did, from all attempts to improve their lot then and there: to find better jobs, to emigrate, to get married. V's refusal to envisage life outside Russia was not caused by any persisting personal tie; the girl he had hoped to marry had perished during the war, and he expressed no longing for any one person left at home; it was rather a supra-individual body that he seemed to have lost and longed to rejoin. The emotional meaning of this loss was made explicit by V's discussion of his position vis-a-vis the Soviet state, or the Russian people *(narod)*. About the DPs' political activities, he had this to say.

"The émigrés cannot hope to enforce their rule when they return to Russia; every political activist wonders in secret if he is going to be accepted over there. If a person loses ties with his people, this in itself is a crime and he must justify himself; he must act so as to earn their acceptance. I am indebted to the people even for my existence and for the way I am; if I were not born in Russia, I would have different character traits, different experiences. And if I left my people in their hour of trial and do not go back for fear of being hanged, it means I am disloyal to them. I can view my staying abroad as a mission and try to do here what people in Russia cannot do for themselves, but it is up to them to decide if they still accept me as their son. We cannot know for sure what people over there think and want; much of what we do is done just to comfort ourselves. If I had been sent here by an anti-Bolshevik organization in Russia, my tie with the people would have been stronger, I would feel I have their sanction, even if indirectly. I want to serve my people, not fight them. I feel justified in acting against the regime that has outlawed me, but the people did not outlaw me."

V expressed similar feelings about his actual family, headed and represented by his father. In the Episodes Test, analyzing the pros and cons of discussing politics in the family, he maintained that after separation there must needs be discussion, the family must know all before deciding whether to take their son back. "They may have grudges, they may say, what right did you have to be over there, not support us financially, even endanger us by acting on your convictions?" While V was still in the Red Army, his father had cautioned him against such a course of action, and he had taken the warning to heart. He himself made the connection between his family's attitudes and his own feelings about his involuntary desertion. "We always had to decide for ourselves what was good or bad and to watch out for the family's reputation; perhaps all I have just told you about the people *(narod)* having to judge me stems from that. . . I never brought shame on my family, even if I avoided this by a mere ruse; when I was captured by the Germans I gave them a false name. If my father will acknowledge me, all these covers will fall away, and if not. . . .But I think he will accept me.''

From the time he first entered school, V had managed with a minimum of support from his family. In his reports of his later life, substitute parental figures, good or bad, did not loom large. Their place seems to have been taken by several friends acting as "older brothers" whom he tried to emulate; to a few of them he could talk frankly, as, e.g., to some good superiors whose standing with the higher authorities was doubtful. He did not dwell on the images of the leaders, of Lenin or Stalin, or Vlasov with whom he had had personal contact; his fantasy productions contained no strong fostering heroes, not any powerful villains. Responding to the picture of a younger and an older man (Card 7), V told a story about a budding revolutionary visiting an old teacher who asks him whether he is strong enough to fight the regime, but for the young man life already means fight or nothing. He decides "that the goal justifies the means, that if one is weak, one can use means that make one stronger, such as robbery, conspiracy, terror. He will commit a terrorist act, be caught and executed".

In V's fantasy, as in his life, the parental functions of fostering, guiding, and punishing were transferred to a supra-individual entity, which was yet highly personalized in his feelings. It was this ultimate collective, whether the Party or the People, to which V looked as a potential source of strength and whose attitude determined not just his external fate but his self-concept as well. But the mythical "People", the elusive hoped-for acceptant collective, were a poor substitute for the Party which can organize positive action. Fighting a suppressive regime, though a worthy cause, was not equivalent to participating in a group effort directed toward constructive goals, not only to fighting. In discussing the issue of violence, V justified war in defense of one's country, but condemned individual terroristic acts; he felt that they made the perpetrator no better than the oppressor and—unless expiated—placed him outside the pale.

E. The Origins of Personality Patterns

In considering V's personal dynamics we must view different periods and levels in succession. The picture he presented during the study was influenced by his reaction to displacement, particularly hard on one of his background and orientation. Yet, essentially, his resignation antedated by many years his uprooting by capture. This resignation, the loss of purpose and zest, was a residue of the unresolved crisis precipitated by the shattering of his early hopes, ideals, and projects. Coming, as they did, in his formative years, these blows may have reactivated doubts about his worth and his competence, latent since childhood.

A sickly child, the youngest of three brothers and the only child among adults or near-adults, neglected and indulged in turn and much teased, V must have felt his weakness and inferiority keenly. The stage was set for his developing and exploiting babyish ways of attracting attention and arousing concern; this may have been his course in his earliest years. In one of the TAT stories he told of a boy who had been poorly served by his parents' indulgence: he never learned to handle difficult situations on his own. This was not to be V's fate; his father's ambition for the youngest son provided a constructive alternative. Given the age difference between him and his brothers, the idea of surpassing their achievements must have been appalling to the child, but he rose to the challenge. Eagerly responding to the stimulation which met his own wish for growth, he mobilized all his energies to overcome the baby and the "sissy" in himself. Both emulating and fighting his elders, he soon rose to a position of leadership in his group. He thus reversed the role he had had in the family, but at some cost to himself. While he developed his capacities in the course of this struggle, there were feelings and wishes he had to suppress and to falsify, thus becoming alienated from himself. He failed to acquire enduring self-confidence. His pride in his success was mixed with doubts: was his manly strength his own rightful possession, had he achieved success through his own assets and by fair means, without pretending, overreaching himself, or disadvantaging others?

The doubts about his own strength and value must have been enhanced by doubt about his father, who had prompted him on his upward course partly in self-aggrandizement and whose own strength, goodness, and wisdom did not stand up during his alcoholic period. V could not be certain of his father's integrity nor of his real attitude to his son. Besides, the father had been unable to guide him in the new and ever-changing setting of the Soviet state, a state which oppressed the peasants but offered channels of advancement to their sons. Without ever having explicitly questioned his father's ultimate rightness, V became alienated from him and turned to his brothers and their peers as the more reliable leaders; there was little warmth in his continued loyalty to his parents.

The Party-State "father", acquired in imperceptible stages through the school and through his brothers, seemed to fill all these gaps. Similar to the real father in being remote, in watching its sons from a distance, the Party was supposed to be all-powerful, all-wise, and unselfishly concerned for the people. And, in fact, the Komsomol leaders gave the young people adequate guidance and a sense of personal worth in contributing to the common cause; the recent heroic past of the Party in the revolution and the civil war lent glamor to all their activities. The Komsomol membership gave V a chance for both self-expression and participation; it also had other personal functions. Admission to the Komsomol was a recognition of merit, a vote of confidence; continued membership confirmed a youth's personal superiority and gave him claim to leadership. With this recognition to assuage his self-doubt, V must have felt less driven to compete strenuously and to prove himself in the group. When the conflict over superiority was lightened, friendship and cooperation could flourish.

When the support turned into irrational rejection and censure, V's feelings of worthlessness came to the fore. He gave up the educational plans that would make him surpass his brothers and friends; in a symbolic gesture of renunciation, he chose a career that he felt would serve his country without demanding independent thinking, initiative, originality. V made a success of his choice without, in fact, renouncing the exercise of these functions; he continued his personal search for truth, in partial communication with his comrades. But neither in his subsequent halfhearted participation in the Komsomol, nor in his later work for the anti-Soviet Vlasovite cause, was he able to attain the self-confidence and the wholehearted allegiance to a group and a cause that had marked his adolescence. He continued to act and fight for his ideals, but at a deeper personal level his experiences and his actions were organized by pessimistic expectations and doubt.

F. Evaluation; Function of Ideology

A gifted person with a strong desire to make something of himself, V had thought much, had worked on himself, and struggled hard to recapture and maintain his integrity. Disappointment in communism and subsequent loss of personal direction were typical of the idealistic youths who had allied themselves with the Soviet state only to have their faith rudely destroyed by experience. In more normal times and circumstances the inner conflicts resulting from the vicissitudes of his childhood would hardly have prevented V from achieving a position of social leadership, or substantial success in some professional field. Within the Soviet scene of the late twenties one can easily visualize him as a devoted and successful educator of the type trained by Makarenko who rehabilitated juvenile delinquents by an ingenious combination of individual approach, personal example and the influence of a group of peers; such a pattern might have fitted many of V's personal needs. Several other professional courses might also have been open to him. His case illustrates some of the personal circumstances that facilitate commitment to a strong, ideologically-founded organization sponsored by a one-party state. It also demonstrates the impact such an organization can have on the lives and minds of its members. Disappointment in one group, one ideal, one party would not have to result in a generalized discouragement if other groups were present to which one's allegiance could be safely transferred.

A word remains to be said about the personal function of V's basic ideological convictions. His belief that individual self-expression and service to a group or cause are compatible and even complementary was a genuine personal philosophy. It resulted from his hard-won insights into significant aspects of human existence and it expressed his personal longings. But this ideology was neither a simple reflection of V's own uncomplicated propensities, nor a means by which his personal conflicts could be fully resolved. Doubting himself and others, he did not find it easy to reconcile self-expression with service in his own feelings and actions. The recurrent conflict of these two trends provided the dynamic force for continued active concern with ideology. A normative solution evolved on a plane of thought became a substitute for a working personal one. V was an ideologue, and as such not unlike the artists of his TAT stories. An ideologue, too, engages in creative work through which he reaches out to humanity, but this activity itself removes him from the common people, placing him on a higher level. He may have to forego the satisfaction of simple unmediated participation in other people's lives. He, too, may prove a misfit living in a different world.

An ideology that functions, in part, as a substitute for the solution of personal problems can be put to many uses. When, during trying times, V succumbed to feelings of personal nothingness, he was able to summon up his belief in the unique value of the individual and to get some reassurance and comfort from it. The belief that he was, in fact, not an isolated unit but a member of totality—the Party, the Russian people—often helped him over the feelings of personal loneliness. Occasionally he used his beliefs to conceal his motives from himself—citing, e.g., the interests of the group or the cause to justify his wish to control others and his irritation with interference. Magnify this mechanism a thousand times and you get an ideological dictator. In V's case these distortions contributed to his feelings of duality, of incomplete integration, but they were not strong or persistent enough to undermine rationality and social contact. More often than not he used his beliefs constructively. When he reminded himself that he was responsible for his actions, or made himself consider the possible justice of another's claim, admitted a fault or accepted the unavoidable frustration of a compromise, he effectively used his ideals as a means to guide and redirect his actions.

Chapter 4

PETER – AN ANTI-SOVIET FIGHTER

A. Life History

Peter, aged twenty-seven (born in 1923), the son of a dekula-kized well-to-do peasant, had lived for years under threat to his life, had had many narrow escapes and experienced severe suf-fering. He was caught in the turmoil of war when he was only seventeen and a student at an agricultural technicum. Eventual-ly he joined Vlasov's Russian Army of Liberation and spent most of the war years fighting. After the war he suffered many misadventures and barely escaped forced repatriation; his life did not become relatively stable and secure until shortly before the time of the study. He was, however, still barred from im-migration to the United States because of having been in the German-sponsored Vlasov's army. He was married to a German woman, had two children, and struggled to make a living as a journalist and as a printer. All these vicissitudes never reduced P to the state of mere pawn. An intelligent man of great vitality, he was a very active participant and often a leader in the events into which he was drawn.

a. Childhood

Peter was born in central Russia, the oldest child of a peasant who during the NEP period left the village commune for a sep-arate holding and considerably raised his income within a few years. During collectivization, when P was six years old, his father was sentenced to five years in the forced labor camps in the north. It was winter when the family was thrown out of their home; in the unheated makeshift shelter the younger son died of pneumonia. Soon the mother, too, was sentenced to a period of forced labor in a nearby community; P and his one-year-old sister remained in the care of their grandparents, who

109

managed to keep them alive through the period of famine. His brightest memories from that time are of his mother's secret visits at night; she took great risks to come every week to see them and bring them food.

The village ostracized the family. When P started school, he was neglected by the teachers, persecuted by the children as the son of an "enemy of the people", rebuffed in all his attempts to reach out for companionship; his former friends refused to talk to him. Yet he loved school, attended it eagerly in any weather and avidly absorbed what he was taught. He met persecution partly by accepting his enforced isolation, partly by standing up for himself and fighting; he was often defeated and beaten up. Yet, even while being mistreated, he believed everything he was taught in school about the good life under the Soviets. Later on, when his parents returned from exile, he would argue the issue with them.

P did not again make friends until he was twelve years old, but the experience of extreme and prolonged ostracism had not crushed him or made him indiscriminately withdrawn or hostile. One of his American interviewers noted: "The informant never described his isolation with the feeling of tragedy, almost horror, that this description evoked in me." Many of these painful experiences P now viewed as humorous and recalled with laughter. Probably the love and concern of his mother and his grandparents softened the impact of his misfortunes and saved him from feeling wholly bad and unwanted; his own capacity for absorption in the things of the mind must also have served as protection. Some basic optimism enabled him to believe that his father's deportation had been an error and that life was indeed getting better and better just as his teachers said.

When P was eight years old, his mother rejoined the family and moved them from the village to a nearby town, where she went to work in a factory. Here the boy discovered the library and started reading voraciously; when absorbed in books on adventure or travel, he would completely forget the desolate reality. Yet at other times he keenly observed all that went on around him. Seeing other youngsters in the breadlines use tricks that got them double and triple rations, he followed suit; he was quite successful in supplying his family with bread. Such activities brought him in contact with gangs of delinquent homeless children who roamed the streets. In school he frequently engaged in fights, which gradually brought him some respect from his fellows, but he fought only in self-defense. P felt that it was thanks to his mother that he had not become a thief or a "hooligan"; her concern for his development and his future had made a lasting impression on him.

When P was eleven years old, his father returned from the labor camp; his health had been undermined, and he died within a year. His mother, like others in her position, was eager to free her son from the handicap of his "wrong" origin; she conceived a plan of passing him off as the son of an aunt. The execution of this plan required moving him from town to town and from school to school until his identity was lost. This was done; by the time he had finished the seven-year school his new "proletarian" identity was firmly established. P's last years in school were happy since he again had companions; he made close friends with two brothers, sons of an employee's family which accepted him as their own. The three friends, the "troika", shared adventures and mischief, dreams, enjoyment of the outdoors, and even their first romance. They all fell in love with one girl, whom they chivalrously served and jealously guarded from contacts with other boys; yet they were not in the least jealous of one another. P's memories from this period reflected happiness and expansion; his schoolmates nicknamed him "Chapayev", after their favorite hero, a fighter in the civil war. At home he was now "the man of the house", and he tried to assert his adult status without going too far in his rebellion. His affection for his mother and his protective tenderness for his sister continued unchanged; he was good friends with his mother, and the sister worshiped him.

b. Adolescence

P wanted to enter a naval school; he had dreams of becoming a sea captain. This course would have fulfilled his father's wish that he acquire a "good" specialty, i.e., one not involving politics. However, when he finished the seven-year school at fourteen, his mother was unable to provide the tuition for further schooling; she wanted to apprentice him to a shoemaker or a tailor. P compromised by entering an agricultural technicum and working evenings as a shoemaker's helper; he used his earnings to pay the tuition. Summer work took him to several kolkhozes, including his home village; here his father's friends talked to him freely about the past and the present. He also had a chance to compare life in the kolkhoz with his early memories of village life under the NEP. He learned a great deal about the organization of agriculture and of the peasant community, past and present, about the official and unofficial workings of the kolkhoz, and about the peasant mentality. He came to feel respect and affection for the peasants, but he was not tempted to return to the village. For him, as for many others, training in agriculture was merely a device for continuing his education. He completed two years of the technicum and then resumed his original plan; after having passed the entrance examination, he was admitted to a naval academy in the south of Russia.

The village experience contributed to P's change of heart toward the Soviet system. This change was neither sudden nor dramatic. It had been prepared by his reading and by listening to people who had visited the newly annexed countries. Moreover, P had always adhered to his family's values, except for his trust in the good intentions of the Soviet government; he had not radically discarded religious beliefs; he had not joined the Komsomol, although this had been due mainly to caution: an investigation might have revealed his true origin. When his own observations began to undermine the idyllic picture of Soviet life he had formed in school, he rejoined the parental sentiments with ease, perhaps with relief. For a while he continued to oppose his mother's opinions from force of habit or for the sake of argument, but at the age of seventeen he stopped arguing and absorbed her stories of the old times like a sponge. There was little Soviet patriotism left in P by the time the Germans struck; he hoped that the war might serve to liberate Russia.

The German advance quickly reached the vicinity of P's home town. When their home was burned he took a leave of absence from school, moved his mother and sister to their native village, and remained with them, overstaying his leave, until he was forced to join the partisans engaged in guerilla warfare against the Germans. After a winter spent with the partisans in the woods, he escaped with a comrade and once more headed for home. During the trek to his village he went through the worst weeks of his life. Captured by some Ukrainian anti-partisans and held for a partisan, he was beaten into unconsciousness. Only his own presence of mind and the help of a peasant woman who had known him as a child saved him from being shot. He was, however, passed on to the Germans, who subjected him to a routine of daily beatings as well as to freezing and starvation; he was near death and wished for it, and was thinking of suicide. But when a lucky chance offered an opportunity to escape, he seized it and eventually rejoined his family.

P's desertion from the partisan group marked the point of no return: he knew that this action would make it impossible for him to resume his old life in the Soviet Union. He was not yet an active anti-communist. Although consistent with his enmity toward the regime, his desertion had not been a deliberate switch to the other side; he had merely wanted to be with his family during the time of danger. He had no wish to fight on the side of the Germans. His hope was that the war would lead to the fall of the Soviet regime, and that the Allies or the Russians themselves would then oust the Germans. In case of a Soviet victory, he hoped to avoid the consequences of his desertion by moving to another part of the country and once more changing his identity. For the time being, he was content to support his family in the village which, under the distant German occupation, enjoyed relative freedom and autonomy.

But P was not only "an industrious, well disciplined, gifted fellow", as his superiors described him; he was capable of leadership if the situation demanded it. His village was being harassed by partisan actions, calculated to bring down the Germans' wrath on the villagers and to punish them for the minimal cooperation with the German authorities which was necessary for maintaining the community. When the village "elder", who had accepted this elective office because somebody had to, was abducted and tortured to death by the partisans, anger goaded P into action. He organized the village for self-defense and was placed in charge of a fighting group of a dozen men. Other villages joined and the local "army" grew. Thoroughly supported by the population, this group proved very successful in protecting the villages from the partisans. When the Germans learned about it, they drafted the self-defense group to fight at the front against the Russians. Upon recovering from a wound, P was sent through a German officers' school and joined the Russian Army of Liberation. From then on to the time when, as an officer of the First Vlasov Division, he took part in the liberation of Prague, enthusiastically fighting the Germans, he was almost constantly in combat. He was wounded several more times.

c. Leadership

One feature which emerges from the detailed report of the war years that P gave in the special interview centered on the partisans and the Germans is his capacity for leadership and for practical action. He was not yet eighteen when he organized the self-defense group; but, within a year, he was put in command of a company recruited by the Germans from Russian common criminals released from prisons. This company was utterly undisciplined; the men had already shot one officer and forced another to flee. P succeeded in transforming this band into an efficient fighting unit devoted to him. Some of his methods show his understanding of the emotional factor in communication. Before undertaking the assignment, he requested time off for studying the argot of thieves; his free use of it stood him in good stead in his first contact with the rebellious company as well as in the subsequent process of taming and training them. His approach was through reasoning and proving; he convinced the men that training would increase their safety in combat, and he demonstrated his point. Probably even more important for gaining the men's trust was his physical courage, his generosity, and his concern for their well-being. The climax of the initial struggle came when P was shot at in the dark and ordered the sergeant to deliver the culprits. The sergeant finally gave himself up; the tight group code made it impossible for him to denounce anyone else and still hope to live. P gave him a drink and suggested that they let bygones be bygones. This finished the opposition against the "milksop", and from then on P was in control.

His unit became very good in combat, and effective in induc-
ing Russian soldiers and partisans to surrender and to join the
anti-Soviet forces. The news spread that the unit did not threat-
en and coerce prisoners and even helped to resettle the uprooted families of the partisans. The discipline P maintained among
his soldiers was strict but not rigid. He gave in on the issue of
drinking, insisting only that drunkenness should follow and not
precede battle, but he was adamant about looting. He explained his policy in this way: "I insisted with the Germans that my
company should always have enough food. I always stressed it
to my own men that they must not loot, because our strength
lay in the support of the people. Once cut off from them, we'd
be just like the Soviet fighters. Now the people viewed us as
saviors, and I told the men that anyone who looted would be
shot on the spot, no matter how little he had taken." In his
military operations P took many risks, but he tried to reduce
the danger to his men by careful planning and succeeded in
keeping the losses low. His men supported him to such an extent that they staged an uprising when at one point he was arrested by the Germans. When, during one of his postwar intern-
ments, P despaired of his life, it was his orderly who saved him
from suicide. Several of his soldiers accompanied him through
all his wanderings and settled with him in Munich.

It is notable that during his service in the RAL P regarded
this army as relatively independent from their German spon-
sors; he acted on this assumption up to the limits of feasibility,
and even beyond them. He was able at first to exercise a great
deal of autonomy in his operations; he even took the risk of
punishing German soldiers for mistreating Russians. When his
company was ordered to the Western front he refused to go,
maintaining that their only task was to fight the Soviets. He
won his point. P is a good example of a person who hated the
German invaders and all they stood for, and yet found a great
deal of satisfaction in fighting in the ranks of the Vlasov organization.

Conflicts with the Germans recurred but, in spite of punishments and demotions, P remained in the East. He wondered
about his future and often discussed his prospects with friends.
His reports of these conversations show that it was a friend, and

not P, who correctly predicted that the Germans would never permit them to build up a big Russian army; it was the friend who felt that people in their position would not be able to return to the Soviet Union after the war. For all his sound observations and ingenious dealings with reality, P's wishes and dreams played an important part in determining his actions.

In other respects, too, the military career did little to change P's attitudes and interests. The person who interviewed him on that period noted that, surprisingly, he was a rather gentle young man, and that there was very little boasting in his accounts of the incidents in which he figured as hero. His eagerness for knowledge continued through the war years. He observed the events keenly and tried to grasp the complicated relationships in the chaotic reality around him; he even continued to acquire book knowledge, e.g., he studied literature with one of his officers. He kept his concern for his family and tried to see them whenever possible. When the Russian advance once more brought the front close to their village, he visited them and moved them to a safer place. They were aware that this meeting might be their last—and so it was. (P's next attempt to rejoin them failed.) On the return trip P could not stop crying, despite his driver's efforts to comfort him. Then he went on a prolonged drunk. He explained his early marriage by the feelings of loneliness and longing caused by the loss of his family.

d. The Postwar Period

We shall not report in detail the misadventures P had in the wake of the Allied victory, when the Vlasovites were being delivered to the Russians. He was interned and escaped several times, and wandered from place to place in search of safety and work. This was a more depressing period for him than the war years had been. The dream, the cause, the support of the group were gone. Most bitter of all, he was outlawed and hunted by the very "democracies" who should have been his natural allies in his fight for a free Russia. The Allies' misunderstanding of the Vlasovite stand and the general ignorance about the Soviet Union made him feel cut off from his surroundings. Things became better when he got to know some American officers. Together with the little band of his former soldiers who traveled with him, P was taken in by an American detachment, given work in the kitchen and sheltered from the Russians. Later he worked at various odd jobs, perfected his knowledge of type-setting, and took a hand in publishing a short-lived Russian newspaper for which he also wrote articles. He married a German girl after a brief courtship. But P's troubles were not over. His journalistic activities had attracted the Soviet agencies' attention. On their instigation, he was arrested as a war criminal. He spent six months in solitary confinement, waiting for a hearing, desperate and close to a breakdown, yet trying to write down some of his experiences in fiction form. The short stories he wrote during this time he considered his best, and he felt that this activity had helped him to overcome despair. At the hearing he posed as the son of an old émigré, whose participation in the Vlasov army did not constitute treason. He fought a battle of mutual vilification with the Soviet representative and, with the Americans' support, won his case.

This last narrow escape preceded our study by three years. Since then P had come into the clear with the American authorities; however, as peace was still unstable and he was legally barred from immigration to the United States, he still felt threatened and had recurrent moods of anxiety. His immediate absorbing concern was to make a living for his family; he was hard pressed by financial worries and discouraged by his lack of prospects. He had been writing articles on various facets of Soviet life for German periodicals, but this source of income was drying up; he was also trying to establish his own printing press for Russian publications.

Curiosity had led P to become well acquainted with the issues and people in different émigré groups; he was pleased to show to the interviewer who visited him that his guests belonged to different political groups and social classes, to the old and the new emigration. Though he did not take an active part in émigré politics, disliking their strife and disunity, P did not want to withdraw into private life entirely and to give up his dream of returning to Russia. He wanted his children to grow up as Russians, and he wanted to keep close to the anti-Soviet fight. He was watching the growth of anti-Soviet feelings in Europe and in the United States. Every sign of this change filled him with joy; any evidence of continued misunderstanding of the DPs depressed him and made him warier than ever of the undercover work of Soviet agents. His two main political concerns were, first, to make the world realize the difference between the Russian people and the Soviet government and, second, to prevent the Allies from repeating the German mistakes. He welcomed the Harvard Project as a sign of the Americans' real wish to know and understand both the Soviet system and the Russian people; he hoped that its findings would affect our foreign policy. He was particularly gratified that we wanted to learn even about the life of the DPs, and he seriously strove to do his part in "telling the West".

P said frankly that in case of war he would prefer to avoid combat, of which he had had more than his share. He felt that a war was necessary but hoped that, with efficient propaganda, the Russian population and the Red Army could be won over to our side. P advocated a systematic planting of rumors, a pointed abstention from the use of the atom bomb and, above all, a quick demonstration of our willingness to return the land to the peasants. Having been successful in his own agitation campaign among Soviet soldiers and partisans, P felt that he could contribute useful suggestions to the large-scale war of propaganda he visualized in the future. However, he made no attempt to use the interviews for selling any pet projects and gave his ideas only when asked for them.

B. Behavior in the Interview; the Dual Personal Style

P's behavior in our interviews presented a dual picture. Tall, of strong build, with handsome regular features, he was impressive, but not immediately open and obvious. In response to the introductory inquiry about the life of DPs, he delivered a detailed treatise about their fate during the postwar years; he cited episodes from his own life merely to illustrate some of his general points, and he took care to make this explicit. He concluded by expressing his own feelings in a very measured way; he was puzzled and disheartened by some American policies and anxious about the future.

P concentrated on his presentation to the exclusion of personal interaction, but he was obviously concerned about being

understood. At times he expressed this concern in a self-depre-
cating fashion. He wanted to know whether his discussion met
our requirements and whether he had not tired the listener; he
apologized for expressing opinions that might have hurt her
feelings, presumably pro-American; he pointed out that he was
trying to be objective and fair in his judgment, as indeed he was.
He also displayed a self-conscious and formal politeness, characteristic of many of the Soviet officers who tried to live up to
the Western, or "old", standards of "culture"; when he once
relaxed in his chair, he apologized for having made himself
comfortable! Yet the more personal portions of his story gave
us glimpses of a very different personal style; P's formal behavior seemed so much like an ill-fitting suit that the interviewer
ventured to comment on his excessive politeness and to inquire
about its origin. Pleased with the "compliment", he answered
modestly that his father had taught him to be considerate of
others at all times. (Later it transpired that P and his friends
had tried hard to observe and copy the German officers' manners
so as not to commit any *faux pas* at the graduation banquet of
the officer's school.)

As the interviews continued, P more and more often abandoned the self-conscious role of informant for freer and more
personal communication. On the second day the interviewer
started informally, without taking notes, and P, who had just
had some setback in his search for work, expressed his discouragement in a simple personal fashion. After this, he readily
accepted the invitation to tell about his childhood and became
quite absorbed in reminiscences. He vividly depicted the events
and his own feelings, obviously enjoying many of the scenes he
recreated. Whenever something in these stories struck him as
humorous he would laugh uproariously though the joke was
frequently on himself. The vigor of this personal narrative contrasted strongly with the deliberate restraint of his earlier dis-
course; the formal politeness went overboard.

P produced a wealth of material in response to the Projective Questions and to the TAT, but his attitude in these two
procedures was very different. The questions were to him
simply inquiries about himself; he answered them by expressing
and describing his feelings in a simple straightforward fashion.

The TAT, on the other hand, resulted in literary productions, in line with his aspirations to be a writer of fiction. He entered into this endeavor readily; he viewed the task as a test of his literary ability, but this did not hamper the free flow of very revealing fantasy. Yet he obviously tried to choose effective expressions, he almost dictated the stories, and his language became rather stilted, contrasting strongly with the natural tone of the remarks he occasionally addressed to the interviewer.

When P read the typed record of his stories, his first reaction was one of acute embarrassment. He found his products pedestrian, was not reassured by the interviewer's protestations, and was particularly depressed by what he considered breaches of good style. Yet his choice of the best piece coincided with the interviewer's—the description of a morning in the country, the least "pseudo-literary" of the lot. By reading it aloud to the interviewer, P overcame the sense of inadequacy, which he described as a mixture of feeling humorous, ashamed, and sad: "No, I am no writer!" Now he anticipated with pleasure his friends' roaring laughter over the stories.

It seems that of the two styles of expression we observed in P, one appeared when he was task-oriented, achievement-oriented, while the other represented free self-expression in a personal situation. Perhaps these two styles of expressive behavior reflected two foci of personality-integration which themselves were not too well integrated within an encompassing whole.

C. Childhood Experiences and Their Effects

We shall describe the early family situations as reflected in P's reports and in his fantasies and speculate about their relevance to his attitudes, in particular to the "dual pattern".

P's mother seems to have been the most important person in his childhood. Together with his grandmother, she gave love and protected him from external and internal threats. In his memories she appeared as a natural, affectionate person with great inner strength. She could flare up in anger, criticize P's behavior, deny his wishes, but there was never any doubt in his mind about her devotion. In his description of their later relationship, the aspect of friendship, of mutual support stood out much more strongly than that of dependence. P appreciated his mother sensitively as a person in her own rights; his feelings toward her showed also a barely disguised erotic element blended with tenderness. After describing her beauty in fresh, non-stereotyped terms, he remarked: "Now I am talking about her as a woman, not as a mother."

With his more controlled (father) P felt less at ease; he responded with stronger guilt feelings to his calm reasoning and shaming than to his mother's impulsive scoldings. When she had scolded or punished him the incident was closed, the guilt expiated; a mere look of reproach was worse; but it was his father's quiet admonitions that made P plumb the depths of uneasy repentance. The father had wider experience; later, during his year at home after his release, he tried to supervise P's school work and encourage his interests; he was seen by the son as strong and competent. He, more than the mother, made the boy feel that he must rise in the world if he was to fulfill the family's expectations and justify their sacrifices.

P did not remember being afraid of his father, but his fantasies showed a great deal of fear. He had early witnessed quarrels between his parents, caused by the mounting pressures which preceded collectivization, and had sensed, without understanding it, his father's suppressed rage against the regime. These observations probably fed his anticipation of harm at his father's hands. One of P's early memories was that of finding some old-time money and stubbornly refusing to surrender this plaything, despite his mother's demands; his father then told him that if this money were seen his mother would be arrested. P suddenly realized how he would feel if his mother were taken from him. He surrendered the money. This episode must have preceded by about a year his father's arrest, soon followed by the exile of his mother.

P's TAT stories were replete with images of parental figures which displayed sharp contrasts of "goodness" and "badness". When parental images were designated by him as such, they closely corresponded to his descriptions of his own parents as helpful and loving. But disguised as a German foreman, a drunken husband, or the Soviet "fatherland" the "paternal" figure appeared as a murderer; the older woman in one story was a promiscuous exploitative seductress who caused the young man to turn to debauchery and cynicism. The stories involving these destructive figures invariably ended in the young hero's physical or moral perdition. When the parents were seen as good, the stories were still not happy; they centered on the son's guilt. The cause of guilt was sometimes trifling (e.g., arguing with his father), and the strength of feeling out of proportion to the occasion. In other cases the son's guilt was unequivocally related to illicit sex and to actions leading to the father's death. The stories centering on guilt did not result in catastrophe as uniformly as those involving destructive parental images; often the possibility of forgiveness and reconciliation was left open. Yet half of the stories told by P (6 out of 13) ended in stark tragedy. More neutral endings were given to stories in which the hero loses or relinquishes the woman to another. In the two stories with happy endings, the turn from bad to good was marked by the appearance of a child or its substitute (a suspected murderer turns out to be tenderly devoted to a puppy). The only story in which the mood was pleasant throughout had no human plot; it was a description of nature in a village setting.

The stories contained many instances of physical violence and also, specifically, of mutilation which leads to the hero's ruin; in one story he is actually castrated by a war wound. Like many other of his fantasy themes, the idea of mutilation was very vivid and strong in P's thoughts. He repeatedly mentioned his extraordinary luck in having lost no limb in the war. Parting from the interviewer, he decided that she probably had a grown son and expressed the wish that this son would never suffer loss of limb.

P's imaginative productions suggest the classical (Freudian) pattern and are dominated by guilt and by expectation of punishment. This last feature, as also the strong contrast between the good and the bad parental images, is often found in obsessive-compulsive characters. However, in P's fantasies love, sex, and tenderness are not covered up or displaced by aggression; nor is the unusually free undisguised nature of his fantasies typical of the well-established compulsive pattern.

P's parents, as convincingly described by him, did not seem to have possessed traits that might foster or fixate in the child this dual good-bad imagery with its resulting ambivalence. Their behavior to him seems to have been neither confusingly inconsistent nor in any way irrational or extreme. One would expect the son of such parents to have no great difficulty in eventually synthesizing the "good" and the "bad" father into one real and quite acceptable person. Why did P's fantasies at age twenty-seven reflect so vividly the peak of the childhood conflict, with no more than a hint at a workable solution?

It is our hypothesis that the fear and guilt were preserved in P's fantasy because the real events of his life fitted these fantasies and gave them an air of quasi-reality. As a young child he may have dimly wished at times to be rid of the rival and the judge—and his father disappeared into exile; this may have made his guilt feelings acute. And then came the punishment much as his father had forecast it: separation from his mother, rejection by teachers and schoolmates, violent fights and beatings.

The whole threatening and guilt-ridden sequence occurred not once but twice. When, in P's preadolescence, his father returned from exile, the son was glad of a chance to learn to know him better; he talked to us about their relationship in a realistically positive way. However, the other side of his feelings is probably rendered quite accurately in his TAT story about a boy's chagrin at his mother's remarriage: "What do I need a second father for, why did she bring him home? True, I have no father, they tell me he died, but we can live quite well without him." In the next story the good "Uncle Vania" dies at the hands of a villain, the murder being disguised as an accident. In reality, too, P soon lost his father, and a few years later the one relatively happy period of his life ended abruptly; the war brought severe suffering, many brushes with death, and the final loss of his mother.

Though the early fantasies and feelings, reinforced by actual events, did affect P's later attitudes, they did not deprive him of his ability to relate to people, both women and men. His identification was strongly masculine, but he empathized with women very readily. His relation to authority had not become compulsive or stereotyped; he opposed and fought bad superiors but made close friends with good ones, whether Russian, German, or American; he himself had been a strong leader and a "good father" to his soldiers. He had always had close friends and enjoyed wide companionship. His marriage had worked out well, and he emphasized the maternal, protective role of his wife. While he enjoyed her mothering, he valiantly struggled to support his family; he was pleased that he was able to feed them well, if not to provide luxuries. In the interviews P talked a great deal about his wife as a person in her own right, about her past life, her feelings; he related with pleasure instances of his humoring and protecting her. The theme of dominance or superiority did not appear in his talks, nor any evidence of persistent conflict between the spouses, although P talked freely about minor annoyances of family life. He did not present his marriage as ideal, or the security it gave him as absolute; while talking about the proven trustworthiness of his wife, he did not fail to knock on wood, by way of protecting himself against a possible change in her feelings.

It seems that with people to whom P was close, by whom he felt accepted, he could express his feelings freely and enjoy the give and take. Such satisfying interaction was not limited to friends of old standing. Even during the few days of the study, P became more and more at ease with the interviewers. One of them he repeatedly met socially; he enjoyed these occasions and fully utilized the opportunity to talk about "everything under the sun" and to satisfy his "insatiable curiosity" about foreign countries. The interviewer felt that in these informal conversations P communicated much more of his personal thinking and feeling than he did in the interviews.

In one notable way P was not free even with friends—he was often afraid to express aggression, to hurt people's feelings. He told us that he simply could not bring himself, for instance, to get rid of guests who were staying too long. During the war, his sensitivity to the pain of others made it hard for him to visit his wounded soldiers. Just as in his childhood with his mother, P much preferred being scolded by his wife to being given a reproachful look; he felt more hurt by guilt than by punishment.

With strangers—who might dislike him or reject him as inferior—P could not behave naturally, put himself across as a person. He told us how painful it was for him to be made to believe that he was wanted and then find out that this was not so; he would suffer a real shock and quickly withdraw from contact. He was also very sensitive to insult. In an ambiguous situation, uncertain of acceptance, P labored to make himself understood and accepted in an indirect way, as he did with us by drawing an objective picture of the situation of the DPs. He expressed his own feelings through ideological issues, trying to explain and justify his stand, to be fair and objective, and he sought recognition through intellectual achievement. Yet this very effort at detachment got in the way of the personal interaction he craved; it often left him with a residue of sadness and embarrassment.

During the early period of ostracism P relied on achievement to get at least a modicum of grudging acceptance from the teachers; he was sensitized to rejection and developed strongly contrasting responses to acceptance and to ambiguous situations. The experience of literally not being talked to made the problem of communication extremely important to him. Being misunderstood was more upsetting than any mistreatment. P became interested in all aspects of language—dialects, grammar, vocabulary, style—and very concerned about using spoken and written language correctly and effectively. His learning of the thieves' jargon, his activity as journalist and printer, his fictional writings, his interest in propaganda may all be viewed as attempts to reestablish disrupted communication, to make himself heard. The personal significance of dialogue was shown clearly in P's report of his first meeting with the American officer who was to become his friend and protector. When P's orderly unwittingly betrayed their Vlasovite past, the American asked P if he was not afraid of being arrested by him; P replied that he did not think he would do it "because you have already started talking to me and getting interested in me". With communication established, he expected the potential enemy to turn into a friend.

D. *The Dual Pattern*

The duality of P's behavior, the strong contrast between the patterns displayed in different situations, is of no great con-

dual Pattern

sequence in itself; it did not prevent him from establishing the close contacts he wanted, since his strong plea for a personal response got through to the other across all the obstacles. The dual pattern interests us because it seems to be a manifestation of P's inner split, a reflection of the alternating attitudes of self-acceptance and self-rejection. With the first attitude goes emotional vigor and expressiveness, strong empathic response to people and to nature, unselfconscious curiosity and mental activity, and a non-judging acceptance in oneself of a wide range of impulses and emotions. The second attitude embodies the anxious feelings of inadequacy and guilt and leads to determined—but rarely successful—attempts both to express and to overcome them by indirect means, such as intellectual mastery. Let us look at the contrasting ways in which P handled some specific emotional trends depending on which of his two attitudes was dominant.

a. Dependence

P's need for affectional interdependence was embodied most strongly in his wish for his mother, a wish he expressed freely and simply; if he knew he had only a few months to live he would most want to be with her and to be in Russia; his longing for her and for his home had often reduced him to tears and brought him to the verge of despair. He manifested childlike attitudes in other ways also. He told us of his wife's protective mothering which he obviously accepted with pleasure. In responding to the projective techniques, he expressed with gusto his enjoyment of childish pleasures. In the Rorschach, e.g., he conveyed rich and zestful gratification as he described very human bear cubs holding feeding bottles in their paws and playing with a balloon at the same time. In telling of his own children, he empathized with their pleasure in raiding the icebox. He expressed the tolerant attitude typical of Russians toward drinking and getting drunk as a means of finding relief from pain, fear, and anger.

Yet, in some of his sentence completions (which he viewed as a literary task), P implicitly condemned "selfish laziness" and selfish taking as well as the "depraved craving for alcohol" which, he said, slowly but surely undermined a person's capacity for work. Not a very good businessman himself, he felt that desire for enrichment easily led to crime; he was repelled by the DPs' readiness for illegal business transactions, though he understood its causes; with apologies to the interviewer, he talked about graft in some agencies dealing with DPs. P did not pass severe judgment on illegal gains, divide people into haves and have-nots, or emphasize his own honesty. Yet he felt that stealing was worse than hooliganism; and it was looting that, as an officer, he had punished most severely.

Thus, P accepted his wishes for receiving and enjoying support when support was embedded in an affectionate relationship; outside of this context he had a great deal of conflict about these wishes and their aggressive implications. In the familiar world of communication and belongingness, the give and take of mutual support was natural; in the remote world of strangers, to take was to steal. In the latter setting P counteracted his "passive impulses" by engaging in active pursuits. He also tried to deal with them through intellectualization and projection, but these attempts were not too successful; they did not free him from his feelings of guilt. The sequence of first attempting in vain to deal actively with a situation of deprivation and then being swamped by depression is shown in the sentence completion: When he had nothing to eat. . . "and no possibility to get work that would give him a piece of bread to prolong his life, he committed suicide".

b. Anger

In real anger-provoking situations, P had no trouble feeling and accepting his anger and was usually able to channel it into goal-directed action. He knew what elemental fury could do when released into fighting. He repeatedly warned us that, should the Allies repeat the German mistakes, the Russians would turn against them in wrath, that the communist youth would "fight with their teeth". Should this burning fury be aroused, our cause would be lost. When his confident attitude predominated, his healthy respect for the effects of anger led neither to exaggerated fear nor to rejection of this emotion; he merely stressed the necessity of conscious control of this force. P spoke of the Russians' propensity to come to blows over

slights as something regrettable but not leading to prolonged
hostility. He felt, however, that it was the mark of a strong,
"aware" and educated person to control such outbreaks, and he
strove to do so. He told us that in the past he had been very
even-tempered, but since his last prison experiences he occasionally flared up with "wild animal fury" and had to work hard to
control his acts. He described two recent instances of getting
raving mad; one outbreak was provoked by the rude act of a
stranger; the second, by fear of possible harm (on being photo-
graphed by someone in a public place). In the first case he hit
out, but the incident ended in reconciliation; in the second he
came to himself just in time (with a chair raised above his head)
and demanded that the film be destroyed.

P felt some regret but not guilt about such instances of loss
of control, which he described as mere momentary explosions.
He knew he had these feelings but did not consider them expressive of his enduring attitudes, as he did, for instance, his
longing for his mother and his home. He knew that his anger
passed quickly; none of the people or groups he had ever fought,
not even the communists, were viewed by him as personal and
permanent enemies.

Yet P was not as free from conflict about aggression as one
might infer from the above. In the sentence completions he repeatedly accused the actor of some crime against the family, of
hurting them by his egoism and rudeness, of nasty actions
toward his friends. His fear of hurting friends at times prevented
him from asserting himself as he would wish; the annoyance he
felt about this would then be displaced onto some trifles.

It seems that P's conflict was not about aggression as such,
and not about fighting the enemies of the moment, but about
the possibility of violence against friends. In P's fantasy the
parental images, especially his father's, appeared now as good,
now as bad; because of this confusion he was afraid he might
mistake a friend for a foe and thus lose a friend and incur real
guilt. This danger made P at times take a darker view of the aggressive force than the one we have been describing so far. He
talked of the dual nature of the Russian people, particularly
of the peasants, with their equally strong propensity for good
and for evil; he said the government appealed openly to the first

and secretly to the second, to create disunity among the people and divert hatred from itself. He was well aware of the destructive consequences of displaced anger, and of emotion "swallowed and burning you up from inside". This knowledge did not protect him from the feelings of guilt and worthlessness caused by his ambivalent emotions.

c. Achievement

To cope with these self-disparaging feelings P would mobilize his drive for achievement, as a means to prove his worth and win recognition. Aware of his abilities, he identified with leadership, and leadership to him meant the use of rational thinking to guide one's actions. Within this motivational setting of having to prove himself, rather than just be and act, P's wishes for knowledge and self-expression functioned as means for asserting superiority and gaining prestige; his psychological understanding functioned as a means to achieve his goals through "propaganda". Yet this attempt to substitute achievement for the total person seldom resulted in real satisfaction and success. P had been a highly successful military leader. In this role he had been able to combine intensive personal interaction with superior achievement; and the war helped to sort out friend and foe, permitting P to fight without guilt. In more normal times, P might have excelled in other leadership positions, such as that of sea captain, which in his youth he had chosen for himself. Solitary work could hardly satisfy him. His attempts at intellectual and artistic achievement did not bring sufficient rewards. In some of his sentence completions he mentioned anger at those who criticize or ignore the real heroes—but this went with a feeling that the main fault lay in himself. The following completions demonstrate a similar mood.

1. His acquaintances. . ."treated with scorn and pity his speech, his way of thinking, his behavior, which were as untidy and disorderly as he was himself". 2. He was most unhappy when. . . "they disagreed with his arguments, while he felt that everything he said had been thought through and therefore was correct and should be accepted". 3. To lead people. . . "correctly, without antagonizing them, is honorable but complicated and difficult, and besides it is not always rewarding".

There were realistic reasons for this intelligent man's failure to obtain satisfaction through intellectual achievement; his insufficient formal education made him inferior to the "true intelligentsia"; the daily struggle for existence left little time and energy for literary pursuits. Yet it is also true that P constantly undermined himself through his own self-mistrust. This was shown nowhere more clearly than in his attempts at creative writing, which, he told us, caused him much more frustration than the factual surveys for periodicals which he prepared with relative ease. He related, without agreeing with him, the opinion of one competent critic that the first, quickly-written versions of his short stories were always the best. We found this easy to believe, on the evidence of P's vigorous communicative speech in which he often used vivid and felicitous imagery to convey emotional meanings. Yet P felt compelled to keep working on the first draft until the language became elaborate and stilted. The final product bore evidence of P's attempt to live up to some unassimilated standard of literary style, and he himself viewed it with disappointment. In a sentence completion he expressed his admiration for those who "have a talent for language; who freely and easily express their thought, forming beautiful clear sentences without making them needlessly florid". When he submitted some of his stories for reading at a Russian writers' meeting, he refused to read them himself and was too embarrassed even to attend the meeting.

d. Depression

Failure of achievement, and of the adjustive strivings which motivate it, left P feeling worthless and exhausted, a prey to anxiety and despair. He had moments of acute depression leading to thoughts of suicide. In the past, he had actually attempted suicide a few times when acute suffering and death seemed inescapable. At the time of our study he felt that his youthful vigor and hopefulness were gone, that his "controlled, cheerful and energetic" behavior was merely the disguise of a man "wounded by life and nearly crushed". And yet, P's reports of his suicidal attempts also showed surprisingly-quick recoveries from these moments of despair, followed by a tremendous mobilization of energy for an attempt to save his life through

SIMEONE

fight or flight; these attempts succeeded, against great odds. P's performance on the Rorschach Test also revealed an alternation of warm outgoing energetic response with discouragement and abrupt withdrawal. All in all, however, P's high level of energy and performance in our study was punctuated only by a few short periods of discouragement and acute embarrassment. One might speculate that the very experience of "giving up" and giving in to despair, with the relaxation of all attempts at control, liberated P's energies for renewed action. His ability to share his despondent feelings with others also functioned as a safety valve and as a means of overcoming these feelings.

E. Summary: Friends and "The Stranger"

P was a person endowed with high ability and vigorous emotions, whose traumatic childhood and youth had left him with a confused picture of the world, oscillating between the beneficent and the threatening, and with a correspondingly divided, "good" and "bad" image of himself. He tried to deal with this dilemma by reinforcing the positive side; partly by clinging to his hopeful expectations, and partly—more realistically—by establishing closeness with people who accepted him and whom he could trust. In such optimal situations, with belongingness and communication assured, P was spontaneous and outgoing, an impressive and likable person; he accepted and shared his feelings and impulses and used his superior abilities effectively and unselfconsciously.

But neither the happy fantasies nor the reassuring interactions with people alleviated P's anxieties in a radical and permanent fashion, since in each unfamiliar person he had to face anew the "mythical enemy", the residue of his early isolation from his world. In Angyal's formulation, it is *alienness* that characterizes this central figure of the neurotic mythology: he is the utter stranger, unfathomable and unresponsive. The presence of this conception in P is suggested by the fact that his attacks of rage had followed an ambiguous act of a stranger and by his various attempts to promote communication; for example, his "insatiable curiosity" about life in foreign countries served to reduce alienness and to create a basis for understanding. Even so, there could be no complete clarity about another person for P, and because of his underlying confusion he could never be quite certain that he would not strike out against friends. To cope with these anxieties he tried to intellectualize his emotions through introspection and to bolster his self-respect by winning recognition through superior achievement; these attempts were often undermined by circumstances and by his own self-rejection, and their collapse caused brief but acute depressions.

Thus, the most conspicuous feature of P's personality structure was the duality of his attitudes, the striking alternation between direct spontaneous behavior, on one hand, and neurotically inhibited, twisted behavior, on the other. The first expressed hope, competence, and belongingness; the second, doubt and self-doubt, the results of the early ostracism and isolation. These are the patterns of health and neurosis present to some extent in all people; unusual are only the frequent shifts from one to another, neither of the two modes of adjustment being permanently dominant.

In Angyal's conception, "Shifts cannot be expected to occur if, or as long as, the non-dominant pattern is underdeveloped and has a low degree of organization. Consequently the best opportunity for observation of shifts is afforded the therapist at that time in therapy when, the neurotic pattern having been weakened and the healthy one strengthened, both are approximately equal in strength and give marked indications of competing for the patient's allegiance" (10, p. 106). P's life, from early on, had provided him with extreme experiences—of warm acceptance and devoted support on one hand, of rejection and danger on the other—and thus with firm foundations for both patterns. Upon having actively worked on this contradictory evidence in thought and in fantasy, he may have emerged as one in whom both the healthy and the neurotic system are strongly organized. Such people often report "vivid experiences of periodic change of mood and behavior, each mood incorporating one of the two basic orientations" (ibid.).

P delivered more elaborate discussions of ideological issues than our other subjects; he also described in detail the attitudes of different social classes; his opinions and observations are summarized in Appendix B. If we compare what P says about

himself with what he says about the different social classes in
the Soviet Union, we find that he identified his "spontaneous"
pattern with the attitudes of the peasants, and the rational
controlled one with those of the intelligentsia. It is notable that
in his description of the peasants' attitudes he emphasizes their
basic duality.

Chapter 5

VASILII – A DISADVANTAGED WORKER

A. Behavior in the Interview

Vasilii, a twenty-seven-year-old unskilled worker (born in 1923), son of a dekulakized peasant, was drafted into the army at twenty; he fought for two years in the war and spent two more years in the Russian army of occupation in Austria, from which he escaped in 1947, three years before the time of the study. His escape was not premeditated; an impulsive act of his was construed as treasonable and led to Va's arrest; he escaped three times, was recaptured twice, and finally made his way across the border.

Va's life in a large, poorly-organized DP camp was not very different from his prewar existence of a disadvantaged worker. He was still badly fed, poorly clothed; he tried to provide for himself by fishing and stealing; he had been repeatedly detained for fishing without a license. He was repelled by the violent strife of the various national groups in his camp; several times he left the camp to try to "build a life on his own", but he never succeeded. The interview took place shortly after Va's return from Switzerland, where he and his buddy Nikolai had gone in search of work, making a large part of the trip on foot. They had been deported and now considered walking to a city in the north of Germany where they had heard work could be found. Va had applied for immigration to Australia, but his application had run into some snags, and he was doubtful about his chances. Thus, he had no realistic long-range plans; he felt handicapped by his lack of education and skills and deeply discouraged about his future. He saw ahead of him only the same losing struggle with poverty which had been his lot in the past.

Thin, threadbare, coatless on a freezing day, Va cut a pitiable figure when he arrived for the interview; he talked about his past and present "plans" in a depressed, lifeless way. Yet, when

134

the interviewer inquired about his early apprenticeship at a tinsmith's, he came alive and with sparkling eyes described his
work and the technical processes involved; now he looked
young and handsome. He was greatly interested in the American
gadgets the interviewer showed him and volunteered to try and
repair a few broken ones. Once rapport was established it was
smooth sailing. Va talked and responded unselfconsciously; his
interest never flagged. Having no urgent desire to discuss any
particular issue, he moved from topic to topic in a rambling
fashion. Each open-ended question of the interviewer released
a chain of thoughts and reminiscences, the interview frequently
resembling a session of free associations.

Va spoke fast, and his sentences were often ungrammatical
or incomplete; at times his meaning had to be guessed. His fund
of general knowledge was meager and obviously derived from
conversation, not reading; when asked questions about topics
of which he knew nothing, he stated his ignorance simply, without any apparent embarrassment. His thinking was concrete and
not well organized; it bore the earmarks of his rudimentary
schooling. Yet, inarticulate as he was, Va manifested a receptive, keen intellect and a childishly fresh imagination which
surprised and delighted the examiners. He described with
humor and feeling many episodes from his childhood and recounted some of the fairy tales he had heard from his grandmother; he also related parables from the Scriptures, commenting on them with fine understanding. Fascinated and intrigued
by the projective techniques, he became thoroughly absorbed
even in the tasks which he did not find easy, e.g., interpreting
some of the Rorschach inkblots. He soon realized that responses
to these ambiguous stimuli could reveal personal attitudes; he
wished he could hear a dozen different people respond to the
same question or picture.

Va's feelings about the topics discussed, the scenes recalled,
were clearly conveyed but not emphasized; there were no
emotional outbursts, and his general tone was mild. He said he
did not like to think of past misfortunes and tended to forget
them but was willing to recall them if it served a purpose: "If
it is for the Americans to read; when they see what kind of
life we have had, maybe they will help us, will make war on

Stalin." Though his tales and comments expressed discouragement, the mood of the interview itself was pleasant; Va obviously enjoyed the personal interchange. He was eager to hear about
the United States, questioned the interviewer about her own
life, reminisced together with her about the beauties of Russian
nature; this was one of the topics he discussed with enthusiasm.
Pleased with the gift of American cigarettes, he treated the
interviewer to his own. They parted cordially, Va expressing the
hope that they might meet again in some happier future, perhaps in the States: "Here we are poor and cannot offer you
much, but it may be different there." This hopeful note was in
marked contrast to Va's generally pessimistic expectations
 which reflected his past experiences; he had been buffeted
about unmercifully and had suffered privations more continuously than most of the other subjects we studied.

B. *Life History*

a. *Childhood*

Va's early childhood passed in the favorable circumstances
of the NEP period. The third son of a well-to-do peasant in
southern Russia, he was well provided for and somewhat indulged as the youngest and initially sickly child, not expected
to live. He was not overprotected, however, and roamed about
freely with the other village children. Parental discipline was
somewhat erratic and far from severe. The stories Va's mother
later told him of his childhood were affectionate and humorous;
he amused the family with his bright sayings and his tricks, con-
sumed more sweets than the two older brothers together, skillfully hammered nails into furniture. He showed an early interest in mechanical devices and soon became a handy repair-
man.

The maternal grandmother, a member of the household, was
a mine of old folk tales and superstitions; she cured various ills
with incantations. Va listened avidly to the fairy tales she told
him; he still remembered them in detail. He told the interviewer one of the Russian favorites, the tale about "Ivan the
Simpleton", the youngest of three brothers; after many misadventures, thanks to his native wit and to magic helpers, he

secures for himself a princess and a fortune, triumphing over
the brothers who had plotted his downfall. The choice of this
tale may reflect Va's childhood fantasies, although his brothers
figure only slightly in the scanty memories of his preschool
years. The oldest brother (eight years his senior) was fond of
Va; in later years he tried to substitute for his father.

Va's rather idyllic image of his early childhood was based on
his family's reminiscences; his own continuous memories began
with the advent of collectivization and the sharp turn in the
family fortunes. Va was five years old when their property was
confiscated and his father deported as a kulak (he was never
heard of again). The family stayed in the village, now a very
poor kolkhoz; the oldest brother left school to go to work along
with the mother; from then on until Va entered the army he
rarely had enough to eat. The family's plight reached its height
four years later when famine struck. To escape starvation they
left the stricken area for the Crimea where they spent four years,
moving from place to place in a harsh struggle for existence.
The mother worked as a washerwoman in a sovkhoz; the oldest
brother, now married, found work in a different locality. Va
was boarded with him for short periods. Like his brother, he
left school at the age of twelve, after four years of schooling;
he went to work tending pigs. He had done very well in school,
though he put in little work and was handicapped by lack of
books. After the second grade he had spent a month in a children's camp on the Black Sea; his good school record had earned
him this reward, a brief respite from misery. For once he was
well fed and free to enjoy an abundance of new impressions,
new sights and sounds. Va dwelt particularly on the memory of
first hearing a band play and a violinist perform; he loved music
and taught himself to play a crude balalaika which his brother
had made for him, but his wish for musical training was never
fulfilled.

With the exception of this one month, Va's later childhood
was insecure and in part disorganized. The father's deportation
and the mother's employment left him without supervision,
though his mother and brother tried to correct him with occasional remonstrations and beatings. These, however, were
poor substitutes for food; they only caused Va to develop ways

of concealment and escape, not too elaborate or ingenious. The following episode must be typical of many. During the famine Va's mother kept the bread in a locked closet, each person getting one slice a day. To help himself to more Va would climb through a concealed opening in the roof; once he fell and broke things in the closet. Faced with imminent discovery, he ran away and hid in the fields for three days; he was caught by his mother and brothers, but this time he did not receive the expected beating.

In the Crimea Va roamed about with gangs of children, sharing in their games and fights and food-procuring activities; picking up fish on the seashore after a storm, shooting birds, stealing fruit. The children were perpetually chased and frequently caught and beaten. They early started smoking and drinking; once a friend induced Va to steal money from his mother to buy liquor. This was discovered and punished; he never again stole from home but tried to obtain money by other means. In retrospect he felt ashamed of having often deceived his mother and resented her efforts at managing their meager resources. "One lives and learns: when mother told me she had no money to give me I did not believe her. But when, at fifteen, I started living alone I found out how it was with money. I wrote her and told her that now I knew what she had meant."

b. Adolescence

When Va was thirteen years old the family returned to the native village, but this did not improve their lot. Their return coincided with the beginning of the purges during which Va's oldest brother was arrested on a charge of plotting against the government. He was sent to the northern labor camps, from which he returned four years later, prematurely aged by mistreatment and backbreaking labor. The rest of the family remained at the kolkhoz, which was as poor as ever. The middle brother, who had completed seven years of school, was employed as a timekeeper; Va and his mother did farm work. As relatives of two "enemies of the people" they were suspect and closely watched; part of their meager wages had to be spent on subscriptions to government loans and other "voluntary contributions". For Va the misery was increased by his dislike of farm work. Having had no practice in handling horses or in other peasant skills, he felt inferior to the other boys of his age. He decided to look for work in the city and obtained permission to leave the kolkhoz. At the age of fifteen he started for Kiev with no possessions and no money for the fare. He made the trip under the bench of a train car, inside a sack belonging to a friendly passenger; a wooden board had been put into the sack, in case an inspector should test the luggage by kicking it.

In Kiev, after first working as a porter, Va became an apprentice and later an assistant to the tinsmith in one of the shops of a factory. He liked this work, and he liked his foreman, but his earnings barely sufficed to keep him alive. He went in tatters until a friend gave him a pair of used pants; he had no permanent shelter, slept in snatches in friends' rooms, in the parks, in the railroad station. Having no watch, he lived in terror of being late for work. Eventually this did happen, but as a minor he was treated leniently: for three months 25 percent of his wages were deducted. "At that time I earned 170 rubles a month; this left me less than 130 rubles, you couldn't live on that. So I began to steal. I stole roofing sheets from my factory. I hid them under my coat. I sold them to people I knew for some 40 rubles each. But the three months passed, and soon I got a job in a higher category, which paid a little more. . . ." Va's situation improved when his foreman provided him with work on private jobs after hours and he moved to a workers' dormitory. The improvement was minimal, however, and Va saw no chances for decent earnings. The stories from this period deal mostly with fights in the dormitory, with being robbed and being suspected of stealing. Once Va's whole team spent two weeks under arrest on suspicion of stealing a suit of clothes while working on a job. As usual, Va did not lack friends; there were people from his village who helped one another as much as they could; most of his companions, however, were as down and out as he; their main Sunday diversion was vodka.

When the Germans attacked, the factory was bombed; the workers were evacuated to the Don Basin and put to work in a sovkhoz. The front line was getting nearer, but Va and his friends were in no hurry to heed the call to join the Red Army: they awaited the Germans as saviors, expecting them to restore the land to the peasants. When the area was occupied, Va returned to Kiev; from there he started on foot for his home village, through the war-torn countryside; he was on the road forty-two days.

Va had many close escapes on the way, but the most significant event of this trip was his religious conversion. In his early childhood he had been taken to church, but later he had accepted the school's anti-religious teachings and had argued with his mother about the existence of God. On his way home, a peasant woman gave him shelter and food; when they parted, she asked him to take a "letter" which told of God appearing to shepherd boys and telling them that He would soon judge the living and the dead and admit believers to heaven; the reader was requested to pass the message on to nine others and to say the Lord's Prayer daily; he was promised joy in the near future.

Va described his reactions as follows: "This woman tried to lead me to God, and I already had a longing to believe. At first I made fun of the whole thing, but she said: 'Take it, sonny, it doesn't weigh much.' I took it, but I still didn't believe. But then I thought of the dangers surrounding me and I said to myself—who knows?—and I made nine copies of the letter. Just then it happened that a man was shot by the Germans for having no identification papers; I had spent the night in the same place and I had no papers either, but they did not take me. So I started reading the letter more often. When I got home, the churches were being reopened but I did not go. I had a strong wish to go, but I was ashamed: we had been taught that for the young it was shameful to believe. . . .Back at home everyone was after us—the Germans, the partisans, the police. I was hiding from the partisans who wanted me to join them; once when they came I climbed up on the roof; they took a couple of shots but did not get me. Later, when fighting in the war, I always carried the letter with me; when comrades made fun of me I would say I just kept it as a souvenir of that woman who had helped me. I was wounded many times but never severely; I was not maimed. And later, in all my escapes, some power kept me safe always; it could have been chance if it had been just once or twice. . . . I did not know any prayers, I just read the letter instead. I started going to church only here, in Germany. At first I didn't know how to behave, how to cross myself, but now when I am in church I feel at home. Everything is old and interesting and beautiful: the singing, the ritual. Once I opened the Bible—it opened on Parables, and I started reading. Since then I have reread the Bible several times. I like the Parables best, about how we should love and help one another."

For about two years after rejoining his family Va shared their precarious existence under the Germans, who proved to be "worse than Stalin". Although mostly leaving the peasants to their own devices, they periodically engaged in punitive actions against people suspected of communism or of helping the partisans. Once Va spent a week under arrest expecting to be shot; having been pressed by the Germans into guard duty, he was accused of negligence which resulted in a prisoner's escape. On the whole, however, he managed to avoid involvement with either of the warring sides. The kolkhoz had been dissolved; Va's family joined forces with a few friends in working the land as a small commune and eked out a meager existence. Va made use of his skills; out of metal scrap he made crude pails and sold or exchanged them; he also made vodka from bread or beets, bribing the German authorities to close their eyes on this illegal activity.

Va's first affair with a woman falls into this period. He met the girl through a comrade, being too shy at the time to approach girls on his own. When mutual attraction developed, Va asked the girl if she had been involved with his friend; she denied it, falsely, and the affair barely missed ending in tragedy. On discovering the girl's infidelity the friend hit her with a brick and then tried to hang himself; Va arrived just in time to take him out of the noose and revive him. The friend then had a change of heart and told the girl she was free to continue living with Va; "but", Va said, "I did not go with this girl until my friend had found another".

c. Adulthood

When the Russians reoccupied the area, Va had to join the Red Army; he spent two years in combat and two more in the army of occupation. In the army Va was at least clothed and fed, except during the worst shortages. He was in many battles and received a medal for saving the life of a wounded soldier whom he carried a long distance on his back. He dwelt less on the military episodes of that period than on his observations of life outside Russia: "Any farmer in Germany lives a thousand times better than a well-off person in Russia. Here you see bicycles in front of every house; if someone has a bicycle in Russia he is considered rich." Before seeing other countries Va believed what he had been taught in school: "I knew that people in the capitalist countries were exploited and worked fifteen to sixteen hours a day. When the Polish war began we were told that we were liberating the Western Ukrainians from the Polish yoke. But then many Poles came to Russia to work; they all had good suits, and we wondered if they were all capitalists. But we were afraid to talk to them and to ask questions." "At home in the morning you listen to the songs over the radio: 'This is you native land, you own country—here old people get respect, and the road is open to the young.' To hear this makes you feel good, but in reality you live in oppression and misery. I myself never saw the good life."

Va was in the battle of Berlin and was in Prague when the war ended. "The Czechs welcomed us, they threw flowers to us, we felt like liberators, but it turned out differently." For a time Va was stationed near Prague, getting trained in military intelligence. This brief period was probably the happiest in Va's adult life. He enjoyed learning how to read maps and use instruments, to orient oneself in time and space. But there was constant talk about the approaching war with the Allies; "Two wolves can't live in the same lair." The future looked dismal, and letters from home spoke of continued misery. Va's village had been burned down; when he went on a furlough he found his family sharing a mud hut with two others; life was worse than under Hitler. He tried to obtain help for his mother but no help was to be had. Later one of his brothers was arrested; he had been in the Air Force, and Va assumed that he had made an attempt to flee the country.

After his return from leave, Va was employed as a guard in one of the repatriation camps from which war prisoners, slave laborers, and Vlasovites were being shipped back to the Soviet

Union. Here it was most dangerous to disobey orders and to talk to the prisoners; one also had to be very careful about what one said to anyone else. Va's tendency to talk too freely, particularly when not quite sober, had been the bane of his life in the army; to play safe he would spend his free time sleeping rather than with his comrades. Yet what he feared eventually happened. Having asserted that victory over Japan was not due to the American atom bomb, a political officer overheard Va make a dissenting remark to his neighbor. Called to task by the officer, Va, who had been drinking, hit him over the head with a bottle; he was accused of being in the service of the Americans and grilled about his contacts; he escaped from detention and went into hiding, posing as a Hungarian refugee; when he was apprehended he escaped again. During his flight he placed himself under the protection of an Austrian who turned out to be a communist and delivered Va to the Soviet officials. He escaped for the third time and eventually succeeded in crossing the border and entering the British zone.

During the following three years Va failed to organize his life and improve his lot, though he repeatedly tried to find work. He might have found some in Munich, but DPs who had no permanent jobs were not permitted to move there, and he was reduced to a meager and idle existence in a "German Economy" camp. The only advantage of this life over his Soviet past was that he could converse more freely and listen to all radio programs. His attempt to establish a lasting relationship with a Hungarian woman had failed, partly because he could not support her, and partly because he resented her going out with other men in his absence. She failed to mend her ways, and after several quarrels and reconciliations Va broke with her: "I decided I better stick with my comrades for now." At the time of the study he derived emotional support mainly from his friendship with Nikolai and from reading the Bible.

C. *The Pattern of Maladjustment*

Va's anticipation of nonsupport and disaster permeated his responses to most of the projective techniques. In the TAT the themes of threat to life, imprisonment, loss of family, loss of work loomed large. His sentence completions showed the same trend: In Ivan's family. . . "the mother died". His friends. . . "are in exile". When he left home. . . "his family went hungry". When a new director was appointed. . . "nothing changed: people were still being accused and brought to trial". He would do anything. . . "just to survive". When he saw the danger. . . "it was too late". In several Rorschach cards Va saw blood, danger, disintegration. The people in Card 2 are engaged in a bloody battle; in Card 3 their heads and legs have been severed, they are falling to pieces; the animal in Card 8, a tiger, keeps climbing higher, wants to grab and dominate everything—just like Stalin; the human head in Card 9 is Lenin weeping over what he had done to Russia. In his responses to these three tests Va hardly ever anticipated a happy outcome for the hero, and he never anticipated it with certainty; at best the outcome was left open. "Man always hopes for the best, but it turns out differently; it may be prison or starvation for him, anything is possible in our country."

The threats were seen by Va as emanating from the Soviet regime and the conditions it had created; in the TAT alone an explicit or implied reference to the "bad authority" occurred sixteen times. This background of pervasive threat made relationships among people unsafe: "With us people are afraid of each other." Va said he could not understand those who betrayed others and deprived them of freedom; yet, having been a victim of betrayal himself, he knew it was likely. This expectation was shown both in the Sentence Completion Test and in the TAT: He is afraid. . . "of his own friends, that they might report what he said; for instance, if I speak against Stalin, and he happens to be a communist". In a TAT story a man has killed a woman either because she has denounced him or because he had been ordered to. Some friends are trustworthy and willing to take chances, but more often than not they are unable to help; thus the mother in the TAT story cannot protect the son from arrest. References to attempted help are frequent in the Sentence Completions, but the outcomes are usually doubtful: When he saw that others avoided him. . . "he turned to another friend for help". When Pavel did not know how to get out of a difficult situation. . . "I helped him when I could". When a misfortune occurred in John's family. . . "I could not help him in any way".

Effort and self-assertion promise little success; "Our life is such that it is no use trying; hard work doesn't help." If one is offered responsible work one should refuse: "He might make an error and land in prison." Va's test responses reflect only sporadic and halfhearted attempts to assert himself. In his sentence completions passive responses outweigh active ones two to one. Fragments depicting difficult or dangerous situations are completed more often in terms of feeling than of action, with fear predominating: When they criticized his work. . . "he was frightened". When he found out that they wanted to replace him. . . "he knew that prison awaited him". Sometimes the solution is to do nothing: When the instruments he needed were not delivered in time. . . "he rested".

The more positive responses express willingness to try rather than a determined effort: When he had nothing to eat. . . "he looked for a way out". When Sergei received the order. . . "he had to carry it out if he could". When he was advised to follow the example of others. . . "he tried to, if they were doing something good, such as study or work". The boy in Card 1 of the TAT loves music and would like to learn to play the violin, but he will not be able to do so. Later Va amended this: if the boy really wants to, he will master the task; but the discouraged response seems to carry more conviction. Va's image of a hostile or indifferent world went with an image of himself as weak, helpless, inadequate.

Aggression against an all-powerful enemy has as little chance of success as self-assertion, and the consequences are more dangerous. Although Va mentions anger less frequently than fear, in the TAT he repeatedly ascribes to the hero rebellion against oppression or a wish for revenge. However, success of aggressive action is anticipated with some confidence in one story only. On Card 18 a worker attacks the director who has been delivering people to the police; he attacks him from behind, to conceal his identity in case of failure, but being strong and determined he is likely to succeed: "Only a strong man will fight a lion." More typically aggression is depicted as an impulsive act that results from despair and ends badly for the hero: "He may get a term or be shot." But if left unexpressed, these emotions can lead to disintegration. Va interpreted the multicolored fragments of the Rorschach Card 10 as the contents of a man's mind: "all his thoughts, his dreams. . .or maybe his head has split in two"; references to disintegration were frequent in his Rorschach. In the TAT stories, a person may commit suicide if he discovers the hopelessness of his situation or is frustrated in his revenge. Since both anger and despair are dangerous, it is better not to feel their full strength and to avoid situations that arouse them. This solution is indicated in some of the sentence completions: I am most happy. . . "when I am alone—I can rest". His past. . . "there is no need to recall it".

On the conscious level, Va's predominant attitudes towards himself and the world were quite congruent with those revealed by the bulk of projective techniques. He felt both disadvantaged and inadequate, lacking in education and skills; when taking the Rorschach he occasionally commented on his inability to combine the parts into a plausible whole. In accord with his impunitive attitudes, Va did not blame himself for not having acquired specialized skills in the course of his hand-to-mouth existence; yet some feeling of personal weakness seems to be implied in his strongly worded regret: "If only I had studied in time. . .the way I see it now, I should have done anything to get trained as an electrician, even if I had to go naked for years." From Va's stories of his past it is obvious that he lacked neither imagination nor initiative in his struggle for existence, and whenever possible he did stand up for his rights; yet his hopeless outlook may have worked against sustained effort and contributed to his failure to improve his lot.

In his actual handling of dangerous emotions Va seems to have followed, in part, the self-protective design hinted at in his projective responses. His memories of his sufferings were muted and his complaints about the present lacked heat; they were much more moderate than one would expect. Sometimes Va used his understanding of people's motives to diminish his own resentment. Talking about his Hungarian girl friend, he noted her selfish demands but partly excused her: "Of course she was young and wanted pleasure and gaiety, and I was unable to take her out, to go dancing." Still, Va's emotions often got out of hand, particularly under the influence of alcohol, which for him had always been a natural part of sociability. In the Red Army his tendency to talk freely and to strike out verbally or physically in response to attack had made him put deliberate limits on his wish for company and contact.

D. The Pattern of Health

a. The Shifts

Although the maladjustive pattern outlined above predominated in Va's attitudes at the time of the study, his pattern of health was also clearly visible; it did not have to be laboriously unearthed or pieced together from seemingly unrelated items. This pattern came to the fore whenever Va shifted into a setting of positive expectations. His mood and his functioning changed. Gone were the pseudo-optimistic, self-consolatory remarks with which he tried to combat his despondency. The dull or anxious behavior suddenly gave way to alert interest in the topic or task at hand. The most striking shifts occurred when Va was questioned about the two situations in which he had had a chance to learn skilled or semiskilled work, his apprenticeship at the tinsmith's and his training in field intelligence. He became thoroughly absorbed in detailed descriptions of the various operations and devices, freely expressed his fascination with how things are made and how they function. Some of his stories reflected his inventiveness: he had found ways to repair complicated appliances or to make things from insufficient or unusual materials. Implicit in these stories was an image of self as confidently competent, not weak and helpless. A shift to a positive mood occurred also when Va recalled his grandmother's fairy tales or dwelt on the few carefree periods of his childhood. Here his enjoyment of music, nature, adventure found vivid expression; instead of a careworn discouraged man, an outcast, here was an eager sensitive boy, full of curiosity, delighting in new impressions. A similar fresh appreciative interest marked Va's response to some of the projective techniques. Contrary to his expressed sentiment that misery was all that there ever was and could be, the image of the "good life", which he had merely glimpsed, seemed to survive undimmed under Va's pessimism: an image of a meaningful world, rich in opportunities for action and enjoyment.

A striking description of reawakened hope in the "good life" was given in response to one of the TAT cards. To most of the TAT pictures Va responded with stories from the "dark world". He, himself, remarked on this when, presented with a blank card, he chose to project wishful images: a happy reunion with his family, a couple enjoying themselves at a fair: "All your pictures are so gloomy," he said, "let this one be joyful." Yet Card 14—the silhouette of a man at a window done in black and white—struck a different chord in Va's emotions; his groping response grew into genuine personal symbol formation, black and white representing the two worlds. "This man looks at something, admires something. . . .It is night, it is dark . . .but he sees something. . . .This man has been living in darkness, and suddenly a window has opened to the light. . . ." Here Va looked up from the picture with a startled expression, as if he himself had just seen a light, and began to speak in a strong animated voice. "This is as in the Soviet Union; people live in the dark and are treated like cattle and do not know what life can be like. . . .Then he gets to the West, he sees other countries—and he sees the light, a new world opens for him. . . . This may lead to something good: once he has seen it he must try to win this light for himself; perhaps our children will live to see a free Russia."

b. Human Interaction

Va's healthy personality pattern could be seen not only when it was in the forefront: it could also be glimpsed in the interstices, as it were, of the maladjustive pattern, beneath the attitudes that cover and distort it. Va's assets were most clearly and constantly visible in his interpersonal relations, and the simplest way to outline them is to present his responses to the Episodes test. These responses are strikingly different from those he gave to the TAT and the Rorschach, and, to a lesser extent, from his sentence completions; this is a telling comment on the importance of the stimulus in the projective techniques. Unlike the other tests, the Episodes were presented orally, as part of the conversation; this may account for some of the difference. More important probably is the fact that the Episodes focus on interpersonal problems (presented schematically and

neutrally, without specifying the country in which they occur.)
Unlike many other DPs, Va did *not* supply a Soviet background,
nor did he conjure up the dark images he produced so abundantly in the TAT. He became thoroughly involved in the solution of the problems as such, making no mention of the dangers
to which the actors would be exposed in a totalitarian state.
Thus, these discussions highlight his conception of people and
of human interaction in an atmosphere free of extrinsic threats.

No actor in the Episodes is a villain. In stories about conflict,
Va identifies with both parties in turn. The foreman who for-
bids a worker to use a new method of his own (Episode 3) may
sincerely believe that the way he had been taught is the best. In
disagreements on political or religious issues (Episode 7) there
may be some truth on both sides. This wide empathy does not
result in relativism; with the situation sufficiently spelled out,
Va knows who is right. The father who tries to force a voca-
tion on his son (Episode 4) may have good reasons, but he is
wrong to insist: "His choice may be fine, but it is no good for
the son; the son must explain that this would be a waste of
money—if he is not interested he won't succeed." Convictions
aren't always based on reason, but they should and could be.
"Every church claims it is right, but actually children simply
adopt parents' beliefs. Baptists have the right idea; they do not
join their church until they are thirty, when they can use their
own heads and decide what they want." Any conflict can be
settled. "That solution will win out which is really better in
practice, not merely looks good on paper."

To solve a conflict one should approach the other person
directly but not in anger (Episode 6): "If he shouts and attacks them, they can just laugh at him and refuse to discuss it;
he must speak in a friendly way." Both parties must explain
their stand (Episode 5): "He can show them that with his
method they can make the work easier and produce more for
the state. I think he will win them over—they are people, not
stones, they are workers like himself. . . .If it were explained
to me in this way I would gladly accept it." A foreman who
feels that his shop is lagging behind in production (Episode 8)
"should get the workers together and try to find out what is
wrong. Perhaps he himself is at fault, or the work is too stren-

uous for them, or perhaps he is merely imagining that his shop is not doing well. The main thing is to understand each other."

Va realizes that reason does not always prevail: "if the father is kind-hearted, the son can persuade him, but some people will stick to what they have said no matter how wrong they are." A person whose friend hesitates to recommend him for a job (Episode 2) is likely to benefit from a frank statement: "If he sees that even a good friend feels this way, it will make him think; he will improve. But he might also get angry and be worse than before, it depends on the person." Negative reactions are not imputed to any one social role; Va advocates deference to age and experience but does not expect the person in authority to be either more "right" or more unreasonably domineering than the next person.

If the actor is unable to convince the other, he must compromise. When one person's interests collide with those of his group, giving up his stand is actually the proper solution. "If my buddies feel that the norm is too high, I would yield, out of consideration; they are many against one, so why not?" One may have to compromise, even when he is right, as a way out of an impasse, for expediency: if the father refuses to finance any training except the one chosen by him, the son should agree; he will be better off than without any. But expediency is not the only or the main issue. Va assumes matter-of-factly that harmony must and will be preserved. "If they do not accept his idea he will have to accept theirs. There has to be unity."

The Episodes demonstrate that, with the background of threat removed, Va felt in direct rapport with people; he viewed conflict without anxiety, anticipating no dangerous consequences, no basic disruption or isolation; his participation in groups and relationships was unproblematic and natural.

These assumptions are borne out by Va's accounts of his life. He mentioned many people who tried to lighten his burdens or to protect him from blows: an old Tatar who prevented a gang of Tatar children from robbing him, a friend "from my village" who gave him some clothing, the foreman who trained him, the Hungarian inmates of the camp who carried on a bitter feud with the Russians but did not count him among their "enemies". Even those who harassed and deprived him were no villains. Within his pattern of maladjustment, when oriented toward threat, Va used his impunitive stand to avoid danger, but at the core of this forgiving attitude there was a genuine sympathetic understanding of others. Telling of a man who denounced others for money, he added that this man had no work and went around in tatters. Va once asked a soldier who had killed and raped in Germany why he had done it; the man said he was drunk and gave in to his wish for revenge—the Germans had killed his family. Va related this with understanding. Asked about his personal enemies, he said he had never had any; when hiding from the partisans he had *felt* as if they were his enemies, but actually they weren't. Most people kept quiet about his fresh remarks, and he suffered no bad consequences: "Once when I was drunk I joked 'Kill the Yids, save Russia' (an old anti-semitic slogan), but this Jew was a good man, he did not report me."

Va chose friends with whom he could have a mutually supportive close relationship. His experiences of group living in miserable conditions made him reject the enforced closeness of a dormitory or a camp: "There is no place where you can talk frankly—everyone can hear you; sometimes it is pleasant to have company, but not with all this fighting and stealing. . .". Va himself stole from strangers but never from friends; once he was suspected of this and did not rest until he had proved his innocence. His stories abounded in instances of help he had received and given, sometimes at great risk to himself. When he realized that a grenade was about to explode, he tried to protect a buddy before taking cover himself. His helpfulness was not limited to close friends; he had helped in the escape of a man threatened with arrest for stealing, though they became friends only later. Va did not emphasize his responsiveness to the needs of others, but clearly this trait formed the core of his positive self-image, while the negative image centered on his lack of determination and competence. In his sentence completions the actor wants his friends "to be like him, to be helpful"; people consider him "a real human being: he helps people; they know he has a conscience".

We have seen that within the framework of pessimistic expectations, Va regarded aggressive actions and feelings as dangerously self-destructive; outside it, when his attitudes were organized by confidence, his feeling about physical aggression was quite relaxed. As he put it in one of the TAT stories, "it may end badly for him" only "if the man whom he wants to fight is a communist". He was not afraid of fights; they had been far too common in the groups he had traveled with in childhood and adolescence. He admitted he was quick to strike out and often regretted it later; he tried—not too hard—to control his temper and succeeded to some extent: "I have never hit an old man; once a man in the camp hit me in the face and knocked me down, but I did not hit back, though my friends made fun of me for that. He was old, and my hands are very hard—I could easily injure a person. Fighting is silly. I usually try to stop fights in the camp."

Va was not given to bearing grudges or planning revenge. When the Germans occupied his village, the Party members were afraid that he might denounce them in order to avenge his relatives, but he did not: "What is past is past, and it would not have brought my father back." Nor did he denounce a certain Komsomol member whom he strongly disliked. "What good would it have done? And this way we got a lot from each other; he became my best friend, we did things together and shared everything."

c. *Religion*

Va's basic convictions about the foundations of human life found expression in his religious beliefs. What he had experienced on his way home through the chaos of the German invasion was a gradual emergence of faith; his account of this process clarifies the personal meaning of his conversion and the factors that contributed to it.

After repeated escapes from danger, many displaced persons came to believe in God, or in some supernatural power, or in their lucky star. When Va decided to copy and pass on the letter with "God's message", he was testing a possible protective device. He told us that his faith was based on the positive outcome of this test: he had escaped death and maiming during the war and after. But his new faith did not remain isolated from his life and his other convictions, as is often the case with this kind of "converts"; it helped to order and stabilize his central attitudes and values. Va's conversion must have made connections with some earlier vital experiences. About the nature of these experiences we can only speculate. His accepting and reading the letter before he had any thought of its possible usefulness was obviously a response to the woman who had befriended him. His earliest religious impressions had come from the women of his family. He had watched his grandmother pray and occasionally accompanied her to church; her absorption in prayer had strongly impressed him. His mother had countered his school-inspired atheism with the simple assertion "God exists".

The "longing to believe" which preceded the crucial episode must have had many personal roots. It embodied Va's hope to escape all the dangers and to live. It may have expressed his wish for the security of his early childhood, when he was well provided for, when his father was there to protect him, when he had a home and felt at home in his village. Whatever the antecedents, belief in God came to mean for Va belief in the existence of a benevolent world order, holding out the promise of the "good life" that had always eluded him. This belief was a real factor in protecting him from extreme despair, from giving up the struggle. When he was accused of treason Va realized that if he were sent back to Russia he might end his life in a labor camp. So he persisted in his attempts to escape against great odds: "When I was escaping and hiding I felt no fear, I had only one thought—to get out and live. And I felt as if some power protected and sustained me."

Having made good his escape, Va began to attend church and to learn about religion. Gradually he overcame his embarrassment at being a stranger in church and not knowing how to behave. He came to enjoy the beauty of the service: "Now when I am in church I feel at home." His religious feelings were strengthened when he discovered the teachings of Christ. He was so struck with the Parables that he practically learned them by heart. He was eager to know more about Christ as a person and was looking for books about him. In the interview he recalled some of Christ's miracles and his words on hypocrisy: "He told us to look at what people do, not at how much they pray." But, above all, he stressed mutual help, love, and forgiveness: "Christ's teachings are true, if we followed them there would be no wars, all countries would share what they have."

Religion for Va expressed human interconnectedness and guaranteed ethical order. Communism pretended to serve this function, but it stood revealed through its deeds as a distortion and denial of moral order, motivated by lust for power. "Communism is a wonderful idea, but in actual life it does not work. To work for this idea, to live as it requires, a person needs strength and faith; but they have rejected God and conscience, and without conscience people act selfishly, forgetting the common good. If Stalin believed in God he could not be so cruel, he would not murder people so wantonly if he knew that God sees it. That is why they decided to do away with God, so they could dominate the people more easily."

Religion was a personal but not a private affair for Va. At first he was held back from fully revealing his new convictions by the feeling that religion was not for the young; they should not share the unenlightened beliefs of the older generation. But his fear of ridicule did not quite prevent him from trying to argue his views even while he was still in the Red Army; after his escape he freely shared his thoughts on the subject with anyone who would listen. His religious convictions created no barriers between Va and his atheist or agnostic companions. He had not been able to convince his best friend, Nikolai: "He cannot bring himself to believe, cannot get away from what he was taught in school." Va regretted the difference but accepted it with equanimity.

E. The Origins of Vasilii's Dual Pattern

Va's early childhood cannot be reconstructed in detail, but it would seem from the data we have that the relationship to his (mother) was central during those years and that he was soundly confident of her affection for him. Even during his disorganized later childhood, his mother, though unable to give much time and thought to her youngest, was often enough perceived as responsible, concerned, and cherishing. He reported that she had sometimes tried to teach him better ways by admonishing him and had prevented his brother from punishing him more severely; she had appreciated his help in the family's struggle for existence; they could talk and joke together in spite of her worries. In line with this conception of her as warmly sympathetic, some of Va's TAT stories depict maternal women, both mothers and wives, who try to protect the man from danger or from his own dangerous agression: "If she succeeds all may end well for him yet." If the motherly woman cannot help the hero, it is because of her own helplessness in the face of overpowering odds.

Yet the image of the mother is not without flaws. Recalling the later years of his childhood, Va depicted his mother also as punishing and depriving, denying him food and money. All the episodes of this kind that he brought up were directly attributable to the extreme conditions of the family's life. Later Va came to appreciate the hard realities his mother had had to face and felt ashamed of having resorted to wheedling and deception to get what he wanted. The belated understanding did not entirely dissolve the negative image, a residue of the lean years which began at the age of five. Asked about his mother as a person, he mentioned her frugality first of all; at another time he contrasted her "stinginess" with his earlier experience of his father's generosity (during the times of plenty). The view of the woman as depriving may have intensified Va's realistic doubt of ever finding a woman who would give without stint and willingly share with him a life of poverty and insecurity.

Given Va's history—the early loss of a parent and of security, the subsequent unremitting hardships and periodic danger to life—his discouragement and maladjustment need no explaining; the image of a threatening world was firmly rooted in his overall experience. What *does* need explaining is that the positive world image, doubtless formed in his early years, was so strong and so readily available. His positive orientation to life was not buried under a complex structure of devices evolved in order to deal with the consequences of a rigidly pessimistic outlook on the self and the world; Va's outlook was not rigid and there were few defensive distortions in his thinking and acting. Depression and wholehearted hopeful involvement seemed to coexist in close proximity; an observer of one phase found it hard to believe ten minutes later that he had the same person before him. It was also hard to decide, even after a longer period of observation, which of his two orientations was currently dominant in Va. We placed him in the "seriously maladjusted" group on the basis of his responses to the two projective techniques which we used to obtain scores of adjustment for all respondents: Rorschach and Sentence Completion. This classification, however, did not do justice to the total picture observed during the study or to Va's past history. Our other "seriously maladjusted" respondents were more severely disturbed.

The particular form of coexistence of health and maladjustment developed by Va can perhaps be accounted for by two interrelated factors in his past. The first pertains to the time and the nature of the initial traumatization, the second to a measure of continuity between the happy and the miserable periods of his life.

Va had been spared in his early childhood; this circumstance was probably crucial. When the blows began to fall in his sixth year, they came from outside the family group and were not aimed at him or his family alone; many of his early companions were similarly affected. He was old enough to sense these impersonal aspects of the painful changes, even if he could not understand their causes. Sharing the experience of misfortune probably cushioned the blows and—what is even more important—counteracted the generalization of the trauma: a good many friends remained friends, he was not alone, and the world was not *all* hostile. According to Angyal, "no event can be considered traumatic unless its effects on later behavior are generalized beyond the particular situation in which they originated ....Generalization is...essential for the genesis of neurosis; it is involved both in the formation of the neurotic organization and in the shift by which it gains dominance" (10, pp. 119-120). This opinion is shared by many.

When privation became the order of the day, the survival of the hopeful "good life" image founded in his early experiences must have been facilitated by Va's trusting relationship with his mother; its positive core persisted through later years. Although his mother turned into a depriver while he was still too young to perceive her clearly as a *reluctant* depriver, he sensed

M
o
t
H
E
R

at least dimly that her attitude toward him had not changed. This continuity in the affection of a significant adult made the change from security to deprivation a partial, not a total, affair; it was a bridge from the bad world to the earlier good one. Had Va experienced his mother's ungivingness as a complete reversal of her earlier attitude, confusion and ambivalence would have been the result. These were not a part of Va's outlook. In spite of his discouragement, the negative features of the world he was familiar with did not color *all* his expectations; he expected bad things to happen only in the contexts in which they had actually happened in the past. True, the threatening context had predominated in Va's life; this was reflected in the frequency with which he anticipated harm. Nevertheless the negative expectations were not always there and not unchangeable. The positive conception of human relationships survived in this man not as a mere hope but as a conviction which had effects; together with nature, music and fantasy, friendship early became for Va a source of genuine satisfactions, and this source never dried up. His openness to these experiences saved him from becoming embittered, even if his strivings for physical comfort, for competence, and for independence were continuously thwarted, with the brief periods of respite or success only underlining the privations. Last but not least, Va had been able to find in the Christian religion an outlook confirming his own basic convictions; this outlook strengthened his hopes and gave meaning and stability to his insecure life.

Chapter 6

NIKOLAI—A POSTWAR SOLDIER

A. Behavior in the Interview

Nikolai, a twenty-two-year-old soldier (born in 1928), was a relatively recent arrival, having lived in the West for only a year. Drafted into the Red Army in 1948, he had been stationed in occupied Germany and a few months later had escaped to the Western zone. His escape had been prompted by the hardships and dangers of service in Germany, by the rumors about an impending war with the Allies, and by a chance exposure to a Voice of America broadcast. These experiences and the difference between the standards of living at home and abroad had increased his bitterness against the Soviet state, which had refused to provide for him as an orphaned child: he had been forced to drop out of school and go to work at the age of twelve. While being transported across Russia with other draftees, N had seen the devastation wrought by the war. An indelible impression had been made by hundreds of ragged children begging for bread at every train stop. N, who had been supporting his younger siblings, fully shared the feelings of the married draftees: if this is what happens to the children of the "defenders of the fatherland", why serve and fight?

The recent arrivals did not have the benefits of the DP status and were excluded from the better camps. N lived in a large camp which housed refugees of many nationalities and provided for them very poorly. His occasional excursions into the outside world had failed to land him a job; his application for immigration to Australia was in its early stages. Some of his companions hoped for war as a chance to fight the Soviet regime and to return home, but N did not share their hopes. He had no one in Russia whom he longed to rejoin, and he harbored no strong feelings for the mother country as such. Of a realistic and

158

critical turn of mind, N was not given to wishful thinking; he was not optimistic about the anticipated war of liberation. His views on the issue made him unpopular among his Russian companions, even suspect to some of them; this caused him to withdraw from political discussions. He reserved his frank thoughts for a few trusted friends; together they tried to improve their lot and speculated about their future.

In the interview N did not dwell on his current troubles, nor did he use it to vent his bitterness against the Soviet regime. Taking part in the study was for him primarily an opportunity to earn some money. He wanted to be a good informant and tried to compensate for his ignorance of general issues by relating his own observations and anecdotes heard from others. His straightforward presentation was full of precise detail. He was particularly well informed about consumer goods: the shortages, the prices in different years, the postwar black market. N took some pride in his memory and in his clear formulations: he asked the interviewer if she could tell from the way he spoke and wrote that he had attended school only four years; and, indeed, he showed a good deal of natural intelligence and did not give the impression of an "illiterate" person. N felt he had another asset for the job of informant: his status of "Recent Defector". The interest in the recent arrivals shown by the Allied military agencies had caused some DPs to falsify the date of their defection, in the hope of being singled out for paid interviewing. N made it clear that he was the genuine article. He proudly displayed his military boots, pointing out that he was still dressed Russian-fashion. Rather short, of a strong compact build, he was neatly dressed and had the bearing of a soldier.

Though he at first emphasized the "objective informant" attitude, N entered easily into discussions of personal topics and memories. He related a series of tragic events in his family in a calm detached tone—a convincing demonstration of his avowed inability to express strong feelings; at the death of his near ones he had experienced intense emotional and physical reactions but had been unable to weep. On the other hand, he recalled with gusto and humor the hunting adventures of his childhood; he also enjoyed telling of tricks he used in his struggle for survival, e.g., to outwit the German police and

evade arrest for fishing without a license. His stories of people
were not lacking in judgments, but these were expressed in
moderate terms and qualified by comments on the causes of
the actions in question. In the Rorschach test N was unable to
produce or accept any but geographical and symbolic (Soviet-
related) responses; the rest of the projective tests he handled
easily and well, presenting much personally relevant material.
In the TAT, he usually started with describing the picture, an
approach typical of the uneducated, then offered some tentative interpretations, though he sometimes refused to commit
himself to a plot or an outcome. On Card 20, for instance, he
felt that since the man's face was not visible there was no way
of telling his mood or thoughts. Significant "projective material" was brought out in conversations. At one point N related
the plot of *A Hero of Our Time*, a romantic novel by Lermon-
tov, which he knew almost by heart; he strongly identified with
the disillusioned hero who pursued and abandoned women.

Though sober and self-contained rather than effusive, N was
in good rapport with the interviewer; he asked a few personal—
but not too personal—questions and increasingly enjoyed the
conversation. When on the second day he was given the choice
of the topic, he chose to talk about girls; he told of having been
almost forced to marry at sixteen, narrated his other affairs of
that period, and commented on the present unhappy love affairs of his friends; he had observed much marital discord arising from the frustrations of the refugees' uprooted life. At the
end, he remarked that he could have told more about his relations with girls if such matters were not out of place in talking
to a woman. Then, with some slight encouragement, he decided that since the interviewer was no longer young, it would
be all right to tell her in writing. A few days later we received a
long manuscript entitled "About my Life", recording the love
affairs of his adolescence, all of them centered on an intense
power struggle, "the battle of the sexes". These episodes, however, were only a background for the central story of "Nikolai
and Olia", the history of his love for a childhood friend who
had died two years before his escape. He wrote vividly, clearly
and frankly. In the introduction he apologized for not having
been able to talk about this part of his life—he found it very
hard even to write about it.

B. Life History

a. Childhood

N was born into a peasant family in the eastern part of European Russia; he was preceded by three brothers (one of them a half brother, from his mother's first marriage) and followed by two sisters. His father came from a very poor peasant family, his mother from a more prosperous one; her parents were dispossessed in 1930 during the collectivization of farming, but they were not deported. N's parents lived very modestly, with some periods of hardship, but suffered no extreme privations even during the year of the famine. The father's occasional drinking and the mother's wish for better material conditions caused some friction, but quarrels were not too frequent; in N's early childhood the family was a going concern.

N's memories went back to the age of five; till the age of ten when his mother died life appears to have been carefree and satisfying. The mother took good care of the children and was close to them; she would scold and cuff them at times, but reconciliation followed quickly, and they could laugh and banter together. N believed that his mother preferred him to the lazy and disobedient brother who was five years older, but he in turn felt displaced by the sister, two years his junior; he thought that the parents paid more attention to her than to any of the boys. He was closest to the brother who was ten years his senior; this brother had taught him to read and at times gave him advice. However, siblings do not loom large in his reports of these years. His alliance was with a few lasting friends: the daughter of the neighbors and two boys who shared his adventures. His father may have cast a dark shadow over his life; he never mistreated the children but he was strict and his orders were obeyed. He was stern and businesslike when sober, never laughed or joked with the children. N was afraid of his glance. The father, however, was often away from home, working on a lumber team, and the boy was not burdened by any parental demands he could not easily meet. He did his quota of chores, was a good student in school without having to try very hard, and spent most of his time roaming about with his friends, fishing and hunting. The Kama River abounded in big fish; a few times N took a dip when the hooked fish proved stronger than he. When he became older, he and his friends engaged in more dangerous exploits, such as shooting at packs of wolves from trees; their crowning trophy had been a bear.

In the tenth year of N's life the friction between his parents became continuous. Quarrels erupted over the father's spending too much on liquor and neglecting his work, probably because of advancing alcoholism. He no longer was meek under alcohol; he became assaultive toward his wife. His stepson came to his mother's defense, and resentments snowballed rapidly. Then came the catastrophe. The drunken father struck the mother, who was in the last weeks of pregnancy; she died after the premature birth of the child. The child—a girl—survived. Within a year the father remarried. The second wife was young, inexperienced, and in no way equipped to win over and manage the resentful stepchildren, some of them as old as herself. The family disintegrated. The father tried to act as mediator; his own children felt that he gave them support, but his stepson, feeling abandoned and persecuted, took to drink. He soon died from pneumonia, which he presumably contracted by falling into a ditch and lying in the water for hours. N blamed his death on the stepmother's having neglected to take good care of him after the accident. His next older brother, who had been a failure in school and had gone to work in a neighboring town, got into bad company and began to drink and steal; the father brought him home, but after trying out various training programs and jobs he left again, this time for good. The father's drinking increased; finally, after a squabble with his wife, he committed suicide by hanging. She found him, but instead of taking him down she called N, who had sought refuge from the scene at the neighbors. He was the one to take his father out of the noose; not knowing the methods to use, he was unable to revive him. This happened when N was twelve years old, less than two years after his mother's death. Six months later the stepmother also died, as a result of a self-induced abortion.

During these years N lost his early carefree spirit and began to watch his elders with concentrated attention, almost spying on them; he formed a highly differentiated picture of their emotional interactions. He was deeply affected by his mother's

death but found himself unable to cry. Talking about the stepmother he emphasized her inadequacies and tended to blame
her rather than his father, yet he also showed understanding of
her own feelings of inferiority and despondence: she had grown
up as an orphan herself, without guidance and without training
in housework. Though glad to see her defeated by the children,
he had tried to behave correctly toward her; he did not partici-
pate in the squabbles. However, it was during this period that
he developed an extremely negativistic attitude toward his
teacher, flatly refusing obedience and eventually provoking her
into striking him. When he pushed her away, she fell, and he
was told to stay out of school. As this issue was being settled
between her and the father, N had the satisfaction of putting
her on the spot: it was against the law to strike a pupil. When
the teacher apologized he returned to school.

N ascribed his father's suicide to his grief and guilt over the
death of his first wife and the quarrels he was having with the
second wife about the children. He reported, however, that the
father had also been depressed by a physician's warning that he
was quickly approaching alcoholic insanity. N left open the
question of the father's responsibility for the mother's death,
but he freely admitted having felt intense bitterness and even
hatred toward his father for the role he had played in it; and
also, after his suicide, for having abandoned the children to
their fate.

Soon after these events N's remaining brother went away to
a factory school in the Urals, and he was left alone with his two
younger sisters. He applied to the kolkhoz authorities for support
to enable him to remain in the village and complete his schooling. This was refused; his father's suicide had made him a son of
an "enemy of the people" who had refused to live in the Soviet
Union. N had believed everything he had been taught in school
about communism and had rejected his parents' religion, but
he was not attracted by group activities and so had been a neg-
ligent Pioneer. During his negativistic period he had even sold
his Pioneer tie and refused to come to the meetings, for which
his father had been called to task. This rift with the authority
was merely a reflection of the child's unhappiness in the family;
it could easily have been mended. But now abandonment by

the father was followed by refusal of support by the state. The children were to be put in an orphanage. N rejected this plan, left school, and assumed the role of provider and head of the household.

b. Adolescence

After working for a few months in a brick factory, N became the kolkhoz shepherd; with his sister's help, he also cultivated the family's garden plot, the produce of which could be legally sold. The few cattle they owned were slaughtered in the first hard stage of their struggles, but later N was able to replace them and turn them into a major source of income. Alert and observant, he proved to be an efficient worker and a careful manager, always aware of the changing conditions of the war economy; he knew when and where to sell farm produce, when to buy clothing and other necessities. Still, with all his acumen, N would only have eked out a meager existence for himself and his sisters during the war years had he limited himself to strictly legal operations. In common with the other peasants, he was not bound by such scruples, particularly as he felt that the state had treated him unfairly. By keeping his own few sheep in the kolkhoz herd and by bribing his supervisors, he was able to enter as his own many lambs of the herd and to amass a small fortune by raising and selling them. He prided himself on having stored up enough reserves during his three years of shepherding to be able to live for some time without working; he decided to use the time to learn some skill that might eventually permit him to escape the sorry lot of peasant.

N entered a nearby factory as an apprentice of the master electrician in charge of repairs. He quickly acquired the requisite skills; after six months of training, he began to be paid for his work. Gradually his earnings increased; he also did some electrical work on the side, when permitted by government regulations; at times he worked up to 14-15 hours a day, mainly testing and repairing motors and installing new ones in farm and factory machines. This work was demanding, but it was highly needed and valued and consequently well paid; besides N was very interested in it and glad of the chance to learn about new models in motors and in electrical equipment.

By the age of eighteen N had achieved his limited objective; he had exchanged the status of peasant for the much better one of semiskilled worker, and his earnings were good. What is more, he had achieved this without leaving the home community to which he was tied by a strong personal tie, and mainly by his own efforts. He had not been entirely without help. Initially, in managing his household, he had had the help and advice of the family of his girl friend, whose mother had been a friend of his mother. Later his superior in the factory had recognized his abilities, encouraged him, and provided him with extra work. N acknowledged this assistance but took pride in having improved his situation without any support from the state (unless one counts as support the permission to leave the kolkhoz for the factory, which had been granted as a reward for superior performance on the kolkhoz job). According to his report, N had evaded joining the Komsomol even while working at the factory, giving as a reason his family responsibilities and the burden of the farm work. Only when he was drafted did he reluctantly join; refusal might have meant discriminatory placement and treatment.

c. Olia and Other Girls

A large part of N's incentive for vocational improvement came from his wish to prepare a better life for the girl he hoped to marry. His exchanging the kolkhoz work for the factory was preceded by an understanding with his childhood friend, Olia. They had been close friends from their early years; they had started school together, N helping Olia with her lessons. Both were made self-conscious by the families' teasing and hinting at a later marriage; to avoid embarrassment they tried to keep away both from the adults and from the boys and girls, who at that stage traveled in separate groups and ridiculed companionship between a boy and a girl. This exclusion, or self-exclusion, from the group increased the friends' intimacy and mutual dependence. After the death of his mother, N spent much time in Olia's home; here sympathy and attention were showered on him, and here he found refuge from the disturbed situation at home.

After his father's death, when he had started out on his own working career, N began to avoid Olia. He had always thought of her as his future wife; when he saw himself doomed to remain an uneducated poor peasant, he assumed that when she grew up she would reject him as husband and provider. Olia faced him with his withdrawal and asked him to tell her frankly if he had stopped caring for her. N explained; when she replied that she wanted him and nothing else mattered, he believed her. He then took the first step to improve his status; he also made up his mind to help Olia to complete her own schooling. When all the men in her family were drafted and their economic situation deteriorated, N not only helped with the farming, but also undertook to pay Olia's tuition in high school and to buy her all the necessities. At that time the cost of clothing was exorbitant, and N's purchases of coats and shoes for Olia spoke louder than words.

They had another confrontation a year later; this time the issue was not marriage in the future but sex in the present. Olia reproached N with courting other girls, which he was doing more and more openly. He was frank in his reply: he felt strong sexual urges, particularly after spending some time with Olia, and he saw no harm in satisfying them with girls who meant nothing to him. Olia confessed her love and her willingness to give herself to N, but he would not hear of it. An affair would make her a butt of village gossip and cause trouble with the family and the school. He did not want any harm to come to her through him. Both were deeply moved by their mutual confessions, and for the first time ardently kissed and embraced. Olia's trust in N was restored; from then on, though she was unable to suppress all signs of jealousy, she desisted from questioning him about his affairs with other girls.

N said that if he had been a little older he would have sought his pleasures with married women, who were the easiest to approach; but until the age of eighteen he had felt too embarrassed to approach them, so he had courted young girls, which had meant pretending love and, by implication, the intent to marry. This pretense was easy because it was known in the village that N's sister, overburdened with farm chores, was urging him to get married, and he had promised her not to postpone it for too long.

Playacting was not distasteful to N at that time. His detailed written account of his main affairs leaves no doubt that for two or three years he was fascinated by the game of pursuit, seduction, and abandonment. He described his interaction with the girls in terms of victory and defeat, of imposing his will, outwitting the other and proving her a fool; he frankly expressed his pleasure in this game. At times he seemed to realize the compulsive element in this activity, asking himself with some puzzlement why it was that as soon as he had had a girl, another would become more attractive to him. More often he fully identified with this course in his notes, declaring, e.g., that like the "Hero of Our Time" he would never submit to a woman, she must submit to him. In pursuing a girl N would try to arouse her curiosity, to keep up her interest by periodic tactical retreats; when ready to get rid of a girl, he watched for some offense on her part which could serve as an excuse for breaking. Though realizing that it was merely a pretext, N still needed a "good reason", in order to justify his actions to others and to himself. He told the first girl he abandoned that she should be ashamed to complain; being a few years older than he, she ought to have realized his intentions from the start; the girl agreed that she had been a fool. When the second girl he lived with became pregnant he arranged and paid for the abortion and was very attentive to her throughout her subsequent illness. He explained his unwillingness to marry her by the prospect of military service in the near future. The girl's family countered this argument by promises of support and, to the accompaniment of heavy drinking, made an all-out effort to talk N into marrying; he was close to succumbing when a timely summons from the factory helped him to escape the situation.

N described these girls' attitudes, hurts, and actions with objective intellectual understanding, but emotionally he seemed to view them as plotters and schemers; he felt they were out to get something for themselves, since marriage protected them from compulsory work in the forests. Moreover, he seemed to assume that from the start they had wanted to humiliate him. This conception is implicit in the feeling of triumph with which he witnessed their tears; it is also suggested by an episode which has an important place in his report of these affairs. Reality came very close to his fantasy of being victimized when the two abandoned girls met and joined forces. They tried to talk another girl into striking back at N by first seeking his friendship and then dropping him, in the hope that this humiliation would make him less desirable in the eyes of other prospective victims. The plot took shape and the action was carried out at the traditional evening gatherings where the young people of the village met in winter. As a keen observer, N was aware from the start that the new girl's approach to him was not spontaneous. Eventually he saw through the situation; he felt triumphant when, contrary to plan, the girl became genuinely interested in him; this was his chance to turn threatening defeat into victory.

The conclusion of this affair reveals the fears which made N try to gain power over women and to keep them in check. He had succeeded in winning the girl over to his side, and all the signs were auspicious for him; but on the eve of a party which he had promised her to attend N suddenly became afraid that all the observations and reports might have been wrong, that the girl might still want to humiliate him publicly. Without a word to anyone he went to another village and another party, leaving the girl without an escort. In the discussion that followed, he faced the girl with her earlier hostile intentions; when she admitted that there had been a plot, he in turn let her know that he already had a serious commitment to one girl and was merely playing with others; no longer wanting her to get hurt, he advised the girl to forget about him, and they parted amicably enough.

After this episode N lost interest in pursuing the marriageable village girls and limited his affairs to women with whom he could have casual sexual contacts. He now devoted his free time to Olia; they made plans to marry in two years, after she finished high school. In this relationship there was no question of mutual hurting, domination or deception, and its harmony was never disturbed.

A year later, at the age of eighteen, Olia contracted a heart ailment; during the year of her illness she remained loving and calm, though she knew she was dying; she was steadily attended by N and died in his arms. N's world was shattered. During the first days after Olia's death he lost consciousness several times;

for weeks he spent his nights at Olia's grave. Again he was unable to weep; friends feared for his life. To escape his despondency he left the village and went to work in another region, but when the novelty had worn off he again found himself immersed in thoughts of Olia. After a year he returned to his village and his factory job; he also helped his sister to obtain work at the factory.

A year later N was drafted and in another few months he escaped. His escape was not an impulsive act. He had experienced hardships in the army, had seen soldiers try to escape them by self-mutilation, had been repeatedly shot at by German snipers and once wounded when patrolling the border; he had killed one of the snipers. The soldiers were told that these attacks were inspired by the Americans, who wanted to provoke another war and should themselves be attacked at a propitious moment. N had no wish to fight for the Soviet state. His hopes of finding a better life in the West were not fulfilled, but he felt no regrets about his defection. He found some companionship among the refugees and made friends with one man, Vasilii. At that time he was not interested in friendship with women. His grief for Olia was no longer acute, but he felt that his chances of finding the right woman were small in his present precarious circumstances. N's written report of his life ends on a note of doubt and uncertainty: the present is bad, the future unpredictable.

obsessive - compulsive

C. Psychological Dynamics

The psychological dynamics of N's personality, as they emerge from his self-descriptions and from the Projective Techniques, conform in the main to the pattern of the obsessive-compulsive character, with much counter-hostility generated by anticipation of hostility. In the interviews he openly if mildly expressed malicious pleasure in outwitting others; his detailed unemotional descriptions of some hunting episodes from his past and of killing the German sniper showed preoccupation with hurting and destruction. Yet this hostility and the fear associated with it did not undermine N's ability to handle himself rationally and to assert himself adequately vis-a-vis companions and superiors. Although he paid lip service to the traditional peasant maxim "listen to your elders", he actually took nothing on faith. He discussed issues only with close companions; with all others he desisted from trying to persuade them if the first statement of his opinions had no effect. N's nonparticipation in the political discussions of the camp inmates once led them to accuse him of being a Soviet informer, a common suspicion among the refugees at that time. N suppressed emotional protest in favor of a calm explanation of the reasons for his reserve; he also suggested that his accusers communicate with the American agency which had checked his background.

An outstanding feature of N's behavior was the strangling of emotions to the point of inability to feel some of them and to express those he did experience. His life had abounded in tragedies, but his oral report of his past contained few references to feelings and few emotional words; he admitted to strong feelings, such as bitterness against his father, only in response to direct questions. He mentioned no fears or guilt feelings and denied having ever experienced strong embarrassment. Most conspicuous of all was his difficulty in fully experiencing and expressing his tender feelings for Olia, the strength of which is vividly conveyed in his written report. When she had cried and kissed him, taking leave of him before dying, N had gone stiff and numb. It was as if he believed love and tenderness to be more dangerous than any other emotions—as if feeling and expressing them would expose him, defenseless, to pain.

And, indeed, N's realistic, moderate judgments of people and human affairs only slightly disguised his conception of the world as cold and hostile. This image, always close to the surface, came out most clearly in the TAT stories; they dealt with crippled soldiers begging for bread, workers striking but failing to win better wages, people looking in shop windows at things they needed but could not buy. The most frequent theme was that of the proud hero's response to a hurt, such as betrayal or rejection by woman, offensive behavior of friends, refusal or loss of job. He withdraws from the scene or engages in active revenge through a criminal action—murder, robbery, theft; he is apprehended, or he commits suicide to avoid punishment; in some stories he makes a well planned escape. If he is caught off guard he is lost—like the man on Card 18 who has been knifed from behind and is now in the attacker's power "because he has already lost control". After killing the girl he loved so that no one else would get her (Card 13), the man feels repentant and lost, but he will escape just the same. In two stories a well-wisher (the hero's father, a girl) tries to prevent him from endangering himself through revenge, but the hero is firm and will do as he must; in an alternative version of one of these stories, the girl herself is the offender whom the man is determined to leave. There are no stories involving effective help. The story of mother and son (Card 6) is one of the most ambiguous. Pursued for some criminal offense, the son has returned home, perhaps to seek refuge; he is at a loss what to do. The mother is displeased and wants him to leave, though she will be sad when he is gone; it is not clear whether she wants to punish the son and protect herself or is concerned for his safety; the outcome for the son remains uncertain, he either escapes or is caught.

One does not have to go very far to find the sources of these threatening and confusing images in N's life; what we cannot know is whether or not the factors that contributed to their formation had been operative already in his early childhood. If so, all the usual traumas and dilemmas of childhood must have been made more acute and more difficult to resolve by the father's withdrawal from the family, the mother's irritability, the tensions and conflicts between them. These would have made it difficult for the child to uphold the image of both as good parents; one or the other would have been wrong and "bad". If such conflicts and confusions were early prominent in N's mind, they may have fostered his concentration on self-sufficient pursuits and his wish to learn how to master situations of danger. However, if we assume that the father's advancing alcoholism had created, not merely intensified, the disruption in the family, it is possible that N's early years passed in an atmosphere free of traumatizing factors. During these years the neurotic orientation may have been merely a potentiality which existed in him as it exists in every child and which might have remained just that, if circumstances had continued to be favorable. But no matter how early or how late the neurotic pattern was formed, it must have sprung into dominance when reality confirmed the worst fantasies N may have entertained.

The catastrophes in which the family frictions climaxed in N's preadolescence demonstrated to him the mutual destructiveness of the parents—or of the sexes—and the resulting victimization of the children. The mother and the stepmother with her unborn child met their deaths as a result of the father's actions, and the other children were left to fend for themselves. In N's perception, the father and the oldest brother had died because of what the stepmother did or failed to do; and though he never blamed his real mother for his father's death, the thought that she had driven him to drink and violence by her nagging is implicit in his report. His bitterness about having had his childhood cut short and having been deprived of his chance for education was directed at both parents.

These experiences left N with the conviction that he must rely only on himself and survive through his own strength or cunning. He must be on guard, keep his own counsel, closely observe what went on around him so as to prevent potential enemies from gaining control over him; he could do this by avoiding or limiting contact with them, or else by beating them to the post and subduing them. The purpose of such a strategy is survival; any temptation to relax, to trust, to feel tender carries within it the danger of being caught off guard, undefended. Reduced to realistic terms, the danger anticipated by N was humiliation more often than physical attack or material deprivation; for all his self-reliant attitude and his justified pride in his achievements, he was very vulnerable to censure and ridicule. The self-image embodying his feelings of inadequancy was that of an unschooled, "illiterate" person who will never be able to provide abundantly for himself and his family. N was a personable young man and many women fell in love with him, but in talking about his successes he usually ascribed them to some impersonal factor, such as shortage of men during the war, or the girls' wish to get married. He was usually forthright in manner, clear and precise in his statements, and he perceived himself as a firm, determined person; nevertheless, in the sentence completions, the obstacles in the actors' path are often "beyond his strength".

The defensive attitudes which N had built up to deal with

these vulnerabilities and threats were neither very complex nor impermeable. For self-protection and for gaining control over situations, he relied on his intelligence, on observation and inferences. In this context, his intellectual processes were used mainly for exploring external reality, not for concealing by rationalization the contradictory elements of his own attitudes. He was capable of self-observation as well. The inconsistencies of what he called his "contrary character" were obvious and puzzling to himself, at least at times. His mistrust of people was moderated by realistic perception. The story of his affairs shows that he was capable of cancelling his "defense through attack" maneuvers when his fantasy of the malicious intentions of others had been cut down to size by reality testing.

The fact that N had achieved real closeness with a few chosen friends is proof that he was able not merely to check and control but actually to discard his mistrust. The prerequisite for this was clarity about the person, based on thorough knowledge; this underlines the uncertainty which is focal in the obsessive-compulsive character pattern. The contrast between the alien and ambiguous on one hand, and the familiar, "tried and true" on the other, was emphasized by N in many contexts. When he discussed, in one of the tests, the problems of a newcomer to a group, he strongly favored initial caution to guard against hatred or contempt which, he said, were often directed at a stranger; but once they got to know him, he could explain his stand and perhaps win them over. In praising the wisdom of reserve N made an exception for those with whom one is close; it had been safe to tease and argue with his childhood chums— the bickering resulted in no harm or grudges. The arguments with his friend Vasilii he similarly enjoyed, whether or not the differences could be resolved. What was the make of a certain machine gun they had seen? Did the pink blot on Rorschach Card 9 represent Lenin or Stalin? Without weighty proof N did not easily change his opinion, but in a non-threatening situation his need to win the argument was not compelling.

The vital role of familiarity in dispelling ambiguity and uncertainty is made clear in N's account of his friendship with Olia, the one he had "always known". He told us how, after the early unselfconscious stage, the two children started ob-

serving and studying each other and how their mutual understanding increased. N's confession of his affairs to Olia may
also have functioned as a means to test her devotion, and she
was never found wanting. In contrast to all the other girls with
whom he had been involved, Olia had always been for him and
never against him. He trusted her and tried to justify her trust
in him; her acceptance of him as her future husband encouraged
him to take a decisive step to improve his economic and social
status; it is clear from his descriptions that with her he felt
open, self-confident, loving. Marriage might have created some
problems for them, for at least two reasons: sex for N had been
strongly associated with power struggle, and the finality of the
commitment might have challenged his oppositional trends.
However, the fact that their relationship had developed and
stabilized despite the hardships and conflicts of N's adolescence augured well for its future. It seems likely that if this
relationship had continued, N's distrustful and defensive attitudes, developed to deal with the unknown and the uncertain,
would have been softened and partially overcome.

Olia's death destroyed the life course N had mapped out for
himself. He felt that from then on luck had turned against him.
He did not collapse, however, nor lose his ability to give his
trust to a reliable friend, such as the lovable open Vasilii. The
possibility of a close relationship to a woman was left open by
N. He talked about it in much the same way as about the vague
possibility of finding religious faith. It is hardly surprising that
he felt so uncertain about his future. To us, too, it seemed even
more unpredictable than that of our other DPs, though he
shared many of their assets and handicaps. Like Michael, Vladimir, and Vasilii, he had been left without a personal tie and
with little hope of forming one; he was worse off than they in
that interpersonal contact did not come easy to him. This also
handicapped him in gaining the support of a group. On the
other hand, service to a cause was not a prerequisite for his
adjustment, as it was for Michael, Vladimir and Peter; and, unlike all the others save Alexei, he had marketable skills. His
prospects were especially hard to assess because of his youth
and the recency of his loss and his uprooting. One could imagine him rallying once more, as he did after the death of his

Comparisons

parents, and stuggling through to a stable adulthood, to a life possibly limited in several ways but well managed and including personal closeness. But one could equally well assume that in losing Olia he had lost his last chance of belonging with another; that her death had confirmed his expectations of harm to the point where any new attempt at closeness would fail because of anxiety and result in more rigid defenses. If all his hopes dimmed, N could even lose control of his drinking and, like the heroes of his stories, destroy himself by committing some vengeful criminal act. Given his stamina and assets, this was unlikely except in extremely unfavorable circumstances. N's case made us especially sorry that no follow-up study of our subjects was possible.

Chapter 7

COMPARISON OF THE INTERPERSONAL ATTITUDES OF THE RUSSIAN DISPLACED PERSONS AND AN AMERICAN GROUP*

Besides the six men figuring in this book, forty-four other Russian respondents of the Harvard Project on the Soviet Social System were studied by us by means of interviews and of projective tests described in the preface. Comparable test data were obtained from American subjects. In this chapter we shall supplement the case studies by a summary of the test results obtained from the total Russian group of fifty subjects studied by us, the test results of the Americans being used for comparisons.

Detailed comparisons of the test data revealed a number of differences between the two national groups. These differences varied in magnitude for different categories of data, but they differentiated the two groups consistently in the same direction, indicating the presence of coherent patterns. These patterns will be described in terms of interpersonal attitudes characteristic of the two national samples, or, alternately, as attributes of the subjects' "social perception". We view social perception as having both cognitive and emotional components, as including both cognition and evaluation of persons and of personal qualities. In using this concept to interpret the test and interview material, the only assumption we need to make is that the personally preferred cognitive and evaluative categories are operative in the perception of real situations as well as of verbally or pictorially represented ones.

*We are grateful to *Psychiatry* for their permission to include this adaptation of the article by E. Hanfmann, "Social Perception in Russian Displaced Persons and an American Comparison Group," *Psychiatry* (1957) 20:131-149.

The conceptualization of personal traits as attributes or correlates of social cognition represents a departure from the more usual way of handling the data of projective techniques, namely relating them to the motivational sphere either directly or by means of the category of fantasy. We chose this way of ordering the data for two reasons. First, it requires less interpretation on the part of the analyst than do many other conceptual schemes. Second, viewing the subjects' responses as reflecting cognitive and evaluative processes insures attention to the stimulus, to the situation that is being cognized; when responses are related directly to motives, the reference to the specific situation to which the subject responds is often lost, which may result in a loss of significant information. For example, a subject's numerous hostile responses justify characterizing him as hostile, but we learn little about the sources of his hostility unless we keep a record of the situations that arouse it.

The use of cognitive categories was also encouraged by the fact that some of the tests actually demanded a realistic discussion of people's behavior, and that in all tests the subjects themselves tended to consider their task as discovering the intended "true" meaning of an ambiguously represented real situation; only a small minority took the tests as an invitation to give their imagination free rein. Such a reality-bound interpretation seems to be common also in this country among unsophisticated subjects without college education: among the Russian subjects it was prevalent to such a degree that only the more realistic of the TAT cards could be profitably used with them.

The fifty clinically studied DPs, who were our main source of data on the Russians, were all of them Great Russians, that is, included no members of national minorities; they were selected more or less randomly from a much larger group interviewed by the Harvard Project. Most of the DPs had been brought to Germany during the war, either as prisoners of war or as slave laborers; they did not want to return to the Soviet Union mainly because they feared the suspicious and punitive attitude of the regime toward those who had spent some time outside the country.

The American subjects from whom comparison data on most

of the tests were obtained by the members of the Harvard team were, like the Russians, paid volunteers. (Rorschach and TAT data were taken from some earlier studies of comparable groups). The place of birth of half of them was Massachusetts; the rest were distributed fairly evenly between the other Eastern States, the South, and the Middle West. All subjects came from homes where English was spoken, although, in a few cases, not as the only language. They were matched to the Russians, subject by subject, in terms of age, sex, and vocational-educational level. The majority of the subjects in both groups were men between twenty and forty years of age.

A question arises at this point regarding the possibility of selective induction into the Russian group of people of particular types—a point which is essential insofar as one is interested in drawing conclusions about the Russian modal personality from the study of this group. A careful consideration of these people's past histories failed to reveal any weighty factors that would make for such selection. We seriously considered the various possible sources of selectivity and tried to check on them. It has been suggested, for example, that the Russian group might consist of particularly maladjusted or particularly healthy people. The proponents of the first hypothesis feel that the decision to leave one's country, or not to return, might indicate deviancy; the opposite hypothesis is based either on the incorrect supposition that most of the DPs were ideological fighters against tyranny, or on the assumption that only the most robust could have survived the hardships of their existence. We attempted to check both variants of the "atypical adjustment" hypothesis by rating subjects on "psychological health", on the basis of total case history and of certain projective tests (6). This procedure uncovered some differences in the adjustment of the earlier and the more recent and still unsettled arrivals; it failed, however, to produce evidence of any gross upward or downward deviation in the mental health level of the Russian group, at least in comparison with the American subjects.

These findings do not, of course, exclude the possibility that there is some selectivity in the DP group in terms of some less "global" personality variables. Furthermore, there are no systematic data for a clear-cut answer to the question that immediately presents itself when one abandons the level of description for that of generalization and explanation: to what extent are the various psychological traits of the subjects expressive of their "basic", early-formed personality patterns, and to what extent are these traits a function of their more recent experiences, in particular of those incident to their position as displaced persons? For some of the attitudes displayed, the connection with the DP situation is self-evident: thus their eagerness to tell their stories was clearly enhanced by their wish to make the maximum use of this opportunity of both "telling the world about Soviet Russia" and venting their grievances. It may be assumed, however, that the more deep-seated personal attitudes, particularly as revealed in the tests, were less affected by recent experiences. In presenting the findings we shall point out those attitudes which would seem to have a very plausible connection with the subjects' adult experiences; for the rest, the reader must decide whether each attitude described is best viewed as a structural personality trait or as a more recent transformation or accretion.

Sociologically our subjects did not constitute a stratified sample. Almost half of them belonged to the middle educational and occupational levels, such as technicians and minor employees; the rest were divided about evenly between those in professions or managerial positions and those who were skilled or unskilled workers, including a few peasants. Thus, the higher socioeconomic levels were overrepresented, and the lower ones, particularly the peasants, were underrepresented in the group. Yet it should be noted that those test findings which, by comparison with the Americans, are most distinctive of the Russian group were obtained largely from subjects on the lower and middle socioeconomic levels, and are not equally typical of the upper level of the Russian group.

It should, therefore, be borne in mind that the characterization of the Russians' interpersonal relations given below applies only to a slight extent to the members of the Soviet elite, and probably not at all to the top level of the ruling group.

The tests which yielded most of the findings pertinent to interpersonal relations are the Thematic Apperception Test, the Projective Questions, the Sentence Completions, and the "Episodes" reprinted in Appendix A (1). We used selected cards from Murray's TAT (9) and the projective questions of the California studies of authoritarianism (4). For the 100 sentence fragments devised for this study completions were obtained from 100 Russians, including the 50 intensively-studied ones, and from a matched American group of the same size. All test responses were coded under a large number of categories.

For the Russian group we had, in addition to the test data, the material yielded by the clinical interviews and the subjects' behavior in the sessions. Since we had no comparable material for the American group, we did not attempt to code and quantify it, reserving it for individual case studies. However, a description of the Russians' behavior can give us an anticipatory summary of our findings. In the interviews they were not satisfied to assume the passive role of respondents but tended to establish a very personal and interactive relationship with the interviewer. They not only participated in directing the interview by bringing up topics of personal concern, but also asked questions about the interviewers' own experiences and opinions; they clearly wanted from them a participant, personal response. Similar attitudes were revealed through the content of the interviews: in the reports the subjects gave of their lives, past and present, friends, family members, and companions functioned prominently and with predominantly positive connotations. Some of the subjects stated quite explicitly that an intensive interaction in face-to-face groups had always been a "must" in their lives, and only a few gave the impression of being permanently lonely or estranged from their human environment. The majority probably shared the feeling of one of them who had gone through many vicissitudes both at home and abroad but felt that he had met understanding, companionable people wherever he had lived and worked. From all this evidence it may be concluded that the subjects were well able to satisfy their strong wish for personal contact and closeness. If this impressionistic generalization is valid, the more specific findings given below might be regarded as preconditions, or as components, of these people's outstanding talent for human contact.

In presenting the evidence we shall draw on both those test items that yielded statistically significant differences between the Russians and the comparison group and those that showed a similar trend, but fell below the level of statistical significance. Previous publications contain more detailed statistical data (1, 4, 6, 9).

(1) The Russian subjects showed a great deal of interest in people and human affairs. Their perception of others was characterized by richness, concreteness, and a relative lack of stereotypy.

This generalization is based mainly on the quantity and variability of all the Russian test responses. In all the tests the Russians by and large made a greater number of single comments pertaining to human attributes and relationships than did the comparison group. On the TAT they created more characters; in the Episodes they discussed the position not only of the main actor from whose point of view the story was told, but also that of the other participants. Furthermore, their comments usually showed a greater variety of content. This point can be best illustrated in the Sentence Completion Test, for each item of which a separate code was developed containing from ten to fifteen categories. In most of the items the Russian responses were distributed over a large number of categories and subcategories, while the American responses tended to be massed in a few categories, to the relative exclusion of others.

From the qualitative point of view the social perception of the Russian subjects appeared to be very concrete and personal. They discussed people's attributes and situations in vivid, descriptive language, using few concepts of the high order of abstraction to which many American subjects resorted. In proposing solutions to interpersonal problems, they attempted to take into account the particular attributes of the participants, to fill out with concrete detail the bare outline provided in the test stimulus.

For example, in one of the Episodes a child refused to go to school, telling his father that he is afraid of the teacher. The Americans dealt with the position of the teacher in a very uniform way, viewing it as being determined by his social role; the Russians considered a variety of possibilities, depending on the teacher's personal characteristics and situation, his age, experience, and attitudes, and the demands made on him by the state. The participant nature of the Russians' response was even more striking when they considered the situation of the child. Many of the American subjects dealt with the child's problem summarily, either hoping that "once the facts are available everything will straighten itself out", or giving some one simple formula, or charging someone else with the solution: "Perhaps professional aid for the child is called for in this case." They almost seemed to be giving up being parents. The Russian subjects, in assuming the parental role, readily entered the child's situation and considered a variety of possible solutions.

> "The father must talk things over with his son, ask him why he was punished. If he says: 'I am poor in my studies', ask him what keeps him from studying. The father must help him, take care of his needs, of his lacks. He might sit down with the child, ask him what he is lacking. Perhaps the child will say, 'I have no pencils'. Or he might want to have a pair of good pants to wear to school—there are many things he might say."

The subjects proposed to appeal to the child's wish for knowledge by showing him what he could learn in school, to dispel his fear of the unfamiliar by enlisting the help of other children, and to explain to the teacher the child's feelings and needs, enabling him in this way "to reach the soul of the child".

From such treatment of the actors of fictitious situations it may be concluded that the Russians did not view people in any schematic or stereotyped way, but rather tended to perceive them as concrete individual entities, with a variety of personal attributes.

The example given above, besides illustrating this general trend, reflects also a more specific one: the Russian parents' great readiness to get actively involved with the needs and with the guidance of their children. This attitude was also observed by some students of child rearing practices in the Soviet Union (20).

(2) *By comparison with the Americans, the Russian subjects were less apt to characterize and evaluate a person in terms*

of his positive or negative attitudes toward the subject himself;
they were more likely to keep in focus those characteristics
that could be more properly called the person's own.

This point needs explanation. The Russians' social perception, far from being impersonal and detached, may even have
been strongly focused on those properties of the other person
that are of great personal importance to the perceiver. However,
the question of whether the other person likes or dislikes the
perceiver seemed to be less relevant for the Russian subjects
than it was for the Americans, for whom it often loomed large.
The completions of some of the Sentence Fragments brought
out this difference clearly. Of the completions given by 100
Americans to the fragment "Andrew's co-workers. . .", 60 percent contained some reference to Andrew, the most frequent
one by far being "liked him". Of the responses of 100 Russians,
only 20 percent contained any such references; 80 percent pertained to the colleagues' own characteristics, activities, or fates.
Similarly, in completing the fragment "He wanted his
friends. . .", Americans much more frequently than Russians
ascribed to the actor the wish to be liked and esteemed by his
friends. The same concern about their worth in other people's
eyes was reflected in the Americans' responses to fragments
such as, "He was most unhappy when. . .", "Nothing irritated
him more than. . .", "He became very angry when. . .". In each
of these items over twice as many Americans as Russians perceived the negative emotion as being caused by people's rejection or criticism of the actor. When a suggestion of a rejection
by others was given in the Episodes in the test stimulus itself,
the Americans more often than the Russians seemed to assume
some unspecified personal shortcoming in the actor, some offensive characteristic that would make for a global rejection by
people—a situation quite damaging for a person's security and
self-respect.

An overconcern with the other person's opinion of oneself
may well interfere with the perception of those attributes of the
other that make him a person in his own right. It is probable,
therefore, that the Russians' relative lack of concern with their
acceptance or rejection by others was one of the factors that accounted for the richness and differentiation of their perception
of people.

(3) In their perception and evaluation of people, the Russian subjects were interested in feelings and motives more than in achievements, external behavior, and physical traits. Their perception may be said to have been directed toward the dynamic core of the personality rather than toward its more peripheral strata.

This formulation is based on a large number of separate findings. In most test items the Russian subjects discussed the feelings and motives of the actors much more extensively and spontaneously than did the subjects in the comparison group. Thus, in several of the Episodes many more Americans than Russians had to be prodded to discuss motivation by questions such as "Why did he do it?" or "How did he feel about it?" and even with this prodding they produced fewer comments than the Russians. In responding to the projective question about the "worst crime", many more Russian than American subjects qualified their replies in terms of motives, naming for example, "murder for personal gain" rather than simply "murder". Similar observations were made in the TAT and in the Sentence Completions. On the Rorschach the distinctive characteristic of the Russians' performance was the predominance of "human movement" responses, which are assumed to connote inner life, over the weighted sum of color responses; the Rorschach literature seems to indicate that in comparable American groups the typical relationship of these scores is one to one.

Differences in evaluation of human actions were demonstrated by the replies given by the two groups to the projective question about the kind of situations that make the subject feel most embarrassed or ashamed. These replies fall into three major categories: "Violation of moral values", "Inadequacy", and "Violation of conventions and etiquette". More than half of the Russian responses fell into the first category, whereas the Americans made more frequent use of the second and particularly the third category, professing that they felt ashamed of failures and of superficial social faux pas. Both the Russians' stress on ethical values and the Americans' concern with social amenities find confirmation in many other test data. Thus, in completing the sentence fragment "People considered

John. . .", the Russians more often than the Americans talked about character qualities such as honesty, courage, kindness, or their opposites; the Americans much more often than the Russians mentioned appearance and good looks. In the fragment "He admired people who. . .", three times as many Russians as Americans mentioned adherence to ideals, while twice as many Americans as Russians talked about status and success. In fragments that call for negative evaluations, the Russians emphasized failure of ethical behavior, while the Americans frequently mentioned annoying personal habits such as smoking or talking in a loud voice.

Even more pronounced was the difference in the frequency of references to personal competence as demonstrated through successful achievement. The following Sentence Completions exemplify the trend that was prevalent throughout. In the fragment "Alexander considered himself. . .", Americans twice as often as Russians referred to effectiveness and competence and to the personal qualities that underlie these powers for action: intelligence, energy, determination. In considering causes of unhappiness, fear, guilt, and shame, the Americans assigned to failure of achievement a much more prominent place than did the Russians. In fragments such as "He is willing to do anything to. . .", and "I often daydream of. . .", they mentioned achievement, career, wealth, or prestige significantly more frequently than did the Russians. The Americans generally attributed to the actor a great readiness to engage in goal-directed pursuits, as well as in activity per se, such as doing things or going places for pleasure, and they approved of this readiness both implicitly and explicitly. This strong emphasis on activity and achievement may detract from the interest in more inward, less tangible personal moments, such as feelings and motives.

There was less difference between the two groups in the mention of abilities as such than there was in the mention of their use in successful achievement. However, in discussing both abilities and achievements, the Russians often qualified their evaluation by reference to motives and purposes; they also stressed those kinds of performances that are most expressive of the achiever as a person. Thus, in talking about desirable mental capacities, the Russians divided their wishes between intelligence and artistic ability, while the Americans spoke only of intelligence. They hardly ever spoke of technological and athletic achievements as being worthy of admiration; if they did, it was in terms of making some discovery of invention "for the benefit of the people". In naming persons whom they admired, the Russians paid tribute to men of science as often as did the Americans. However, the first choice of the Russian group went to writers and artists, who were mentioned by thirty-three Russians and by only twelve Americans.

(4) People were freely perceived by the Russians in terms of both positive and negative characteristics: the subjects neither avoided evaluations as such nor showed any tendency to overemphasize the positive traits at the expense of the negative ones.

In describing people and human situations, the Russians, by and large, used more terms with evaluative connotations than did the subjects in the comparison group, and they also gave a greater number of explicit evaluations. In most of those sentence fragments the replies to which could be grouped into evaluative and neutral or factual ones, the Americans gave proportionately more neutral replies than did the Russians. Fragments such as "Most of his acquaintances. . .", or "His grandmother. . .", were completed by about twice as many Americans as Russians in terms of vital statistics—place of residence, occupation, age. The Americans responded to the fragment "In Mark's family. . .", by enumerating the family members almost eight times as often as did the Russians. In most of the Episodes fewer Americans than Russians spontaneously evaluated the position of the participants, and in the TAT the Americans gave a larger proportion of inconclusive or neutral—neither happy nor unhappy—outcomes.

Even more pronounced than the difference in the degree of total valuative commitment was the readiness of the Russians to mention not only the positive but also the negative characteristics of people; by comparison the Americans often showed a restraint in their judgment which almost suggested a taboo on any negative characterizations. In some of the sentence completions, the preponderance of the laudatory or optimistic comments in the replies of the Americans was quite striking. Thus, in completing the fragments "Alexander considered himself. . ." and "People considered John. . ." 90 and 80 percent, respectively, of the American subjects made laudatory comments, while the corresponding Russian percentages were 60 and 50. Similarly the fragment "Andrew's co-workers. . ." was completed by some positive reference by 80 percent of the Americans as against 45 percent of the Russians.

When the relationship of the people in question was defined as close, the Russians' tendency for an even distribution of positive and negative statements was less strong. The responses of the two groups to the fragments "His father. . ." and "His mother. . .", although different in many respects, expressed positive attitudes with about equal frequency (in about two-thirds of the cases), and the same was true for "Mark's family. . ." and for "His grandmother. . .". However, in the TAT the Russians, unlike the Americans, did not always paint a positive picture of the father, and in the projective questions they named fewer relatives among the people whom they admired. In completing the fragment "He wanted his friends to. . ." some Russians wished that the friends should be ethically good, should conduct themselves well; the Americans never completed this fragment in a way suggesting that they did not consider their friends perfect.

(5) *Although perceiving negative human traits, the Russian subjects did not show much severity in their judgment of people. Specifically, they were more tolerant than the Americans of impulsive behavior of any kind, of the seeking of sensual pleasures, and of such manifestations of personal "weakness" as wishes for passivity, affectional support, and help from others.*

The general point made above serves to complement and qualify the statement about the Russians' readiness to perceive negative human traits along with the positive ones. The Russian subjects were, by and large, not very severe judges of human foibles; in this sense they were not very moralistic, in spite of the emphasis they placed on ethical character qualities. They voiced strong indignation about certain unethical actions and attitudes, but they accepted a wide range of human impulses and of lapses from the ideally desirable as natural or as hardly avoidable. Even when they vigorously condemned some of a person's actions, they did not give the impression of rejecting him *in toto*, as a person. It should be noted that this description is based on individual case analyses of the Russian subjects and not on a systematic comparison of the test data of the two groups. Consequently this generalization does not imply that the attitude of the American subjects was different in this respect.

The statement concerning the traits of which the Russians were particularly tolerant is also based in part on evidence contained in the case histories. They include many accounts of impulsive acts committed both by the subject himself and by others; instances of striking out in hot anger, of running away in fear, or of attempting suicide in despair are usually recounted by the subjects in an accepting, tolerant way. For some of these attitudes evidence is found also in the results of the projective techniques. Thus, the Russians often mentioned strong emotions, while the Americans, in responding to such stimuli as "When a misfortune occurred in Tom's family. . .", talked more often about using self-control. In discussing the projective question about the best way of spending the few remaining months of one's life, many more Russians than Americans talked about indulging in sensual pleasures—eating, drinking, sex— freely ascribing such wishes both to others and to themselves. When occasionally they expressed themselves as being against overindulgence, either in pleasures or in strong emotions, the terms they used indicated a sympathetic understanding of the very states and actions they proposed to control.

The difference in the attitudes of the Russians and of the comparison group is most pronounced with regard to all wishes and actions that have a connotation of passivity. Just as the Russians did not share the Americans' high evaluation of activity and achievement, they also did not share their rejection of passive wishes and states. For them the receptive states involved in contemplative pursuits, or in receiving affectionate support from others, had no pronounced negative connotation and did not signify personal weakness, as they seemed to do for the Americans. This different evaluation of the passive wishes is reflected in the different contexts in which references to such wishes or states were made by the two groups. The Russians revealed their passive wishes in responding to direct personal questions or to those test items that refer to the actor's conscious feelings and wishes: "In his spare time Bob liked to. . .", "I felt very unhappy when. . .". The Americans gave very few passive responses to such items, expressing instead their preference for activity and achievement; their passive responses were reserved for those items in which no wishes or feelings are mentioned ("When he met with obstacles. . ."), and particularly for those which postulate undesirable qualities. Thus, although the Russians mentioned drinking quite frequently in their discussions, in completing the sentence "Tom's main weakness was. . .", it was the Americans who, with a high frequency, gave the response "drinking". The Russians were quite apt to condone even excessive drinking, considering it as a way to alleviate mental suffering.

(6) The Russian subjects seemed to be acutely aware of the fact that a person's feelings and motives are not always directly reflected in his words and actions, and that alternative explanations must be considered and tested if another's behavior is to be adequately understood.

This generalization derives from two lines of evidence. The first consists of the Russian subjects' preference for certain categories under which persons are perceived and evaluated. In praising people the qualities of sincerity, truthfulness, and frankness were emphasized. These traits were mentioned by them more frequently than by Americans in all contexts that called forth positive evaluations, both in the interviews and in the tests. Conversely, in passing judgment on people's negative traits, the Russians gave prominence to deceit, hypocrisy, and flattery, attitudes which were rarely discussed by the Americans.

The two national groups did not differ as much with regard to another prominent focus of ethical evaluation: that of kindness, helpfulness, responsiveness to others. However, the Americans, if one is to judge from their great preoccupation with conventional friendly gestures and their obverse, did not seem to distinguish clearly between the external act and the underlying attitude, as if assuming them to be one. On the other hand, the Russians' emphasis on sincerity in this context may indicate an awareness that feelings and motives are not open to inspection by others, and that only a person who does not falsify or conceal them can be easily seen for what he is and can be trusted in his expressions of friendliness.

The second line of evidence for the Russians' awareness of the ambiguity of social perception was provided by their already cited tendency to produce a great many comments in discussing human actions, and to consider a variety of possible motives, giving about equal attention to the favorable and unfavorable alternatives. These findings are not limited to group trends, the same tendencies appearing also in the individual records. They were particularly clear in the TAT, which for most of the subjects posed the task of a correct reconstruction of a real situation from the available limited clues. Examples will be given from the TAT record of one subject whose habit of weighing the alternatives was particularly strong and had functioned very adaptively in real life situations. In the test he usually attempted to analyze the preconditions for each "plot" or each outcome he envisaged, looking for clues in the picture—particularly in the actors' expressions—as to which set of conditions was present; he then either decided on an interpretation, or else suspended judgment quite comfortably.

Card 4. (A young woman is clutching the shoulders of a young man whose face and body are averted.) Maybe he is not happy in his family life—maybe his wife displeased him in some way; he does not want to talk to her, turns away. Or else he has had some troubles in his work and came home nervous; his wife tries to soothe him, and he is about to go somewhere—perhaps to ask friends for advice and help. (How will it end?) That depends on what it is and what his friends will tell him; if it is family trouble, it may very well end in divorce.

Card 7. (A grey-haired man is looking at a younger man who is staring into space.) Father and son look at something, or read a newspaper; their eyes are directed at the same spot. From their faces it seems that they do not like what they see—they feel it should not be that way. (What do they see?) Perhaps in the newspaper—like it is with us at home—someone has been convicted and they know this person and that he is not guilty in the matter, but they cannot say a word. Or perhaps this is at a factory—the young man has made a model and the older one is checking it. The younger one is waiting for what he will tell him, whether the work is good or bad. He is glad that he has made it and is being checked, and at the same time he is expectant and anxious. (How will it end?) If he has done it well, he will be praised; if not, he will be told it is no good, and will feel badly. (Which is more likely?) I think the young one will prove right.

Does the awareness of the ambiguity of behavioral signs attested to by such tentative and multiple interpretation constitute an essential, structural aspect of the Russian subjects' social perception, or is it different in this respect from the traits described so far? For this attitude, more than for the others, one must consider the possibility that it has its roots in factors extrinsic to the subjects' personality structures but intrinsic to the conditions of their past lives.

The totalitarian regime to which these subjects had had to adapt confronts the person with severe and often unpredictable dangers: reading political meanings into all personal acts, the authorities not only punish the violation of laws but may also punish any failure in work as sabotage and any deviating opinion as treason. On the other hand, the difficult life conditions and the net of restrictive regulations make it impossible for people to achieve even the minimal goals of existence without resorting to unofficial or illegal ways of doing things and covering up for each other in a network of mutual help—the so-called *blat*. These circumstances promote lying and concealment and at the same time sensitize people to these disguises. The existence of a wide network of secret informers—who, under pressure to fill their own "work norms", may report even a joke as "agitation against the regime"—makes misplaced trust extremely dangerous. Yet, one must also be able to trust, since survival is impossible without mutual help; under these circumstances life and death may depend on correct social perception. If one considers also that the war and postwar fates of most DPs also necessitated both deception and reliance on others' help, it would be astonishing indeed if this schooling in caution had remained without effect on our subjects.

Such effects were actually found; they appeared both in the idiosyncratic, fear-determined responses the subjects gave to those test items that recreated for them some threatening features of their former environment, and in the suspicions they entertained concerning the total American study which was the first enterprise of this kind in their experience. The Harvard group had been rumored in advance to be an agent of the American immigration authorities or, alternately, a Communist agency that might deliver them into the hands of the Soviets. Even though the mediation of the DPs' own organization enabled us to clarify the situation and to enlist volunteers, many of them still displayed an initial suspiciousness which conflicted with their strong wish to tell their story. Yet the suspicions and misinterpretations did not seem to be deeply ingrained: they were easily uncovered and removed as the interviews progressed. Some subjects at first concealed those facts that might be prejudicial in the eyes of the American immigration authorities, such as Party membership, or high rank in the Red Army, or even atheistic views; later, after their trust in the interviewer had been established, they confided this information, even though they were not pressed to do so. In several cases the subjects themselves explicitly corrected their misinterpretations, or their idiosyncratic responses to the test items, showing good insight into their subjective causation; some of them became the best propagandists for our study. All these observations suggest that their exaggerated suspiciousness was a consequence of their life experiences rather than a deep-seated personal attitude. On the other hand, even when their trust in the interviewers seemed complete, and when the matters discussed had no practical implications and evoked no memories of past dangers, the subjects still manifested a lively desire to understand people fully and continued to discuss a wide range of alternative human motives.

From these observations the following tentative conclusions were drawn. The subjects' awareness of the complexity of human motives and of the inward, "hidden" nature of motivation is an intrinsic structural feature of their social perception; in addition, this implicit awareness has been sharpened by their later experiences and focused on the vital issue of people's trustworthiness. This interpretation is consistent with the other findings of the study, insofar as most of the distinctive traits of the subjects' social perception cannot easily be conceived as being aftereffects of some late specific experiences. Furthermore, there is some indication that the tendency to see through the superficies and disguises to the real motives operates also in the subjects' perception of themselves, where it cannot be due to any immediate practical incentives.

If this interpretation is correct, the tendency of the Russians to consider the alternative motives and outcomes may signify a differentiated awareness of the ambiguities of existence, which, when kept within limits, enables the person to view and solve his conflicts within a wider perspective. In perception of others, the admission to awareness of contrasting hypotheses may be assumed to facilitate the assimilation of evidence on both sides and thus result in a more adequate and balanced perception than that developed under one exclusive attitude.

(7) The Russian subjects paid much attention to the situation in which the cognized person finds himself, viewing his life-space in terms of dynamic, motivation-relevant factors. In evaluating the person's total life-space, the Russian displayed a marked predominance of pessimistic expectations.

In trying to predict a person's course of behavior, as in the Episodes, the Russian subjects often specified the situational background in terms of various forces impinging on the person, and varied their predictions according to the nature of these forces. In the two episodes that depict a foreman in relation to workers the Russians anticipated very different degrees of disciplinary behavior on the foreman's part, clearly relating greater severity to the greater threat from above to which lenience would expose him in that situation.

In regard to the evaluation of the environment—of what it has in store for the person—the Russian subjects' expectations were much more negative than those of the comparison group. This was demonstrated not only in relation to specific environmental occurrences, such as a change of bosses, but also in relation to generally characterized life-spaces, such as those set up in the sentence fragments "In his childhood. . .", "His past. . .", "His future. . .". If one omits the neutral completions of these fragments, the ratio of positive to negative characterizations given by the Russians of the person's life-space in these different stages are 1 to 3, 1 to 2, and 2 to 3, respectively. The corresponding ratios for the Americans are 6 to 1, 2 to 1, and 4 to 1.

For the Russian subjects, vital deprivations, losses, and dangers loomed very large in most of the tests. On the TAT these themes ran through stories given to most of the cards. The parents of the hero have died; the family are kulaks and have been dispossessed; there is no money to pay for the son's education and training, no means of livelihood, and starvation threatens; people have been arrested and taken away and are lost to their families and friends. Happy outcomes, while not infrequent, were far less predominant than they were in the Americans' stories.

A review of the life histories of the subjects provides some confirmation for the assumption that their personal experiences colored their expectations. The most uniformly negative evaluation of life-space was given in the tests by those subjects who had been exposed from early childhood to heavy blows and privations—for instance, children of dekulakized peasants.

The difference in the evaluation of the environment by the two groups takes the same direction as the difference in their evaluation of persons; therefore, one might be tempted to subsume both sets of results under some common category, such as a wider range, or a greater polarization of emotions, or the greater pessimism of the Russians. All of these factors may have been present; yet the differences between the Russians' evaluation of persons and of their life-spaces should not go unnoticed. The evaluation of the environment is predominantly negative: in the sentence completions referred to above it was seen as positive, as supporting and furthering the person, on the average, in only 25 percent of completions. Yet in the series of sentence fragments dealing with people the percentage of positive evaluations given by the Russian subjects varies between 30 and 70; the positive and negative statements are made with equal frequency. Some of the disadvantaged subjects who depicted the life-space in the darkest colors were both differentiated and sympathetic in their perception of persons. This clear-cut difference between what one expects of people and of the less personal environment did not hold for the American group, whose real life-space contains no such drastic threats and coercive forces as those reported by the Russians.

The Russians' attention to the motivating situational factors in conjunction with their negative expectations of the environment may be one of the reasons for their relative leniency in judging people. When a person's actions are seen as being determined by vital lacks and by powerful threats, he is partially absolved from blame for the ensuing reprehensible behavior. Thus, in spite of their emphasis on honesty and sincerity, the Russian subjects often condoned cheating, lying, and stealing as regrettably unavoidable under the Soviet conditions of life and did not think of the actor as a liar or thief. If cheating or evasion were impossible, they would condone obedience to repressive authority without justifying this authority inwardly any more than did those American subjects who favored open opposition.

(8) *The Russian subjects' perceptions and evaluations of persons were relatively stable in that they were less affected than those of the Americans by the introduction of the element of interpersonal conflict.*

A listing of the data of all the tests referring to the same role, or pair of roles—father, mother, boss, father and son, husband and wife—revealed that, by and large, the Russians' expectations regarding a given role were fairly consistent from one test item to another. The attitudes of the comparison group varied more widely, showing some reversals from a predominantly positive to a much more negative conception of a given person or role whenever interpersonal conflict was postulated or suggested by the text of the item. As reported before, in the case of neutral stimuli such as the fragment "His friends. . .", the Americans usually gave predominantly positive responses, while the Russians distributed theirs between positive and negative ones. When the item depicted conflict, the distribution of the Russian responses did not differ much from that of the responses to the neutral item, but the Americans' perception of the person in the identical role shifted toward the negative.

Thus, in the TAT picture usually perceived as father and son, the majority of the American subjects described the old man as giving good advice which the son follows or ponders; only one-third of the Russian subjects saw the situation in this way, the rest either viewed father and son as pondering a common problem or the father as dominating or punishing the son. Yet in the episode that postulates a disagreement between father and son about the son's studies, the situation is reversed. Both groups took an equally strong stand for the son, but the Russians combined it with undiminished empathy with the father, while the Americans more often conceived of the father as being unreasonably authoritarian and self-willed, bent on dominating his son. Similarly, in completing the "neutral" fragment "When a man expresses his political opinions, his wife should. . .", a slightly larger number of Americans than of Russians displayed equalitarian spirit, admitting the wife to an active participation in the discussion. Yet, in discussing the episode depicting a husband-wife conflict, the Americans were the ones who insisted on the husband's supremacy and who saw the woman as bent on dominating the man. The most striking reversal was observed in the episode concerning a person in conflict with his co-workers, as compared with the completion of the sentence fragment, "John's co-workers. . .". The latter was completed by the Americans in a much more uniformly positive vein than by the Russians; yet, given the element of conflict, they perceived the co-workers as hostile or indifferent; the Russians' conception of the co-workers was not changed in this situation of temporary disagreement.

The Russians' acceptance of interpersonal conflict as relatively nonthreatening is consistent with their lesser dependence on the good opinion of others and with their previously noted lesser fear of criticism. This attitude also helps to explain some variations in their prediction of happy or unhappy outcomes in the different tests. In the TAT the Russians seem to have responded to the depressive, gloomy tone of the depicted scenes—on which they often commented—by bringing into play their conception of the nonsupportive or crushing environment which meant misery or tragedy for the actors. The Episodes were formulated schematically and factually, and in most of them the subjects were asked to predict the outcome of an interpersonal conflict, the general background of which was left unspecified. To the extent that the Russians placed the inter-personal occurrence within the Soviet setting they perceived in the environment many threatening factors as determinants of the actors' behavior. Yet, insofar as they concentrated on the interpersonal attitudes of the participants themselves, they readily anticipated a favorable outcome of the conflict. As a resultant of these two factors, their total forecasts were no less optimistic than those of the Americans, whose perception of the environment never included equally threatening factors.

(9) *All of the characteristics of perception of others dis-cussed so far seem to apply also to the self-perception of the Russian subjects.*

In discussing the findings in regard to the Russian subjects, one could cite as evidence not only the perception of real or fictitious others, but also some of the subjects' self-descriptions. These self-references, which were given either in reply to the direct inquiry of the projective questions, or in asides to other test responses, or in the life history interviews, were quite sim-ilar to the discussion of other persons, both in their formal characteristics and in the preferred cognitive and evaluative categories. Furthermore, analyses of individual cases have shown that for many of these subjects the attitudes revealed by the projective tests were quite similar to those manifested in their behavior and formulated in their self-descriptions. They appeared to have a fairly easy access to their feelings and not to be given to enduring self-deception to any high degree; as a consequence, they were also able to apply the same standards of evaluation to themselves and to others.

The same general congruence of self-description and of descriptions of others was apparent in the American group, although in the latter case the basis of observation was more narrow, since fewer tests were given and no interview data were gathered comparable to the data on the Russians. As the study included no device for measuring the degree of this congruence, no basis is available for deciding whether or not this feature is more distinctive of the Russian subjects' perception.

(10) *The Russian subjects tended to perceive each person as dynamically interrelated with other people, as an active partici-*

IMPORTANT

pant in relationships and in group life. They accepted this sit-
uation implicitly without feeling much conflict between group-
belongingness and maintenance of personal integrity, a conflict
which was manifested by the American subjects.

This is one of the most clear-cut differences that emerged
from the comparison of the two groups; evidence for it can be
gleaned from most of the tests. The Russian subjects introduced
more relationships into their interpretation of the test stimuli
than did the Americans; for example, more family situations
were mentioned by them in the TAT. In discussing the interpersonal Episodes they did not identify exclusively with the
main actor, as the Americans tended to do, but distributed their
interest more evenly among all participants, including those of
the opposite sex. When they talked about a person in relation
with others, their formulations implied his active participation
both in the maintenance of harmony and in disruption; the
Americans, more often than the Russians, depicted him passive-
ly suffering the consequences of rejection or persecution. In the
episode that suggests the rejection of a person by a group, the
Russians often thought that some unfair action of the actor
toward his friends might have caused their displeasure and that
he could reestablish harmony by clarifying the situation and
making amends; the Americans often proposed that the actor
find and correct some offensive trait in himself entirely on his
own, without any interpersonal communication and action. The
Russians' sense of active participation in interpersonal events
probably was one of the bases of their greater optimism in the
face of conflict.

Even more pronounced was the difference in the emotional
evaluation by the two groups of relatedness versus independence and isolation. Both groups seemed to value relatedness
highly and to reject isolation; however, the Americans attached
to both sides of the dilemma some negative connotations not
shared by the Russians. The latter did not seem to anticipate
isolation as a realistic threat; for instance, they expressed few
misgivings about giving up unrewarding relationships, feeling
that if a friend proves false they "can always find another who
has a better understanding of things". By comparison the Americans showed a greater concern about preserving social harmony

as a means of avoiding the threat of isolation. On the other
hand, close belongingness also has its dangers because it seems
to conflict with the person's integrity and independence. This
aspect was stressed much less by the Russians. For example, in
discussing family conflicts in the Episodes, the Russians, although they sided with the growing children in their wish to live
their own lives, did not share the Americans' feeling that emancipation is a value as such, or that achievement of self-reliance
demands a loosening of family ties. This difference in evaluation
was most striking in the episode about the worker who does not
share the group's feeling that their work norm is too high. The
Russians depicted him as responsive to the needs of his fellow
workers and wholeheartedly approved of his yielding so as not
to endanger their earnings through his superior skills. The Americans felt that his first duty was to stand up for his personal
convictions, yet had great misgivings about his ability to live up
to this standard of integrity. They visualized the group as a coercive force to whom the individual must yield if he is to avoid
rejection or persecution: "He does not want to quarrel with his
fellow workers. The other men maybe live differently, think differently from him, and his relations with them are stressed
severely. He'll eventually go along with them, I think; he is
probably not strong enough to stand on his own feet against
them."

Another striking example of how difficult it seemed to the
American subjects to reconcile individual integrity and close
personal ties was provided by their discussion of the conflicting
wishes of marital partners concerning their respective jobs and
the place of residence they entailed (Episode 9). They were involved in this episode much more personally than were the DPs.
We had not expected American men to insist so strongly on
their prerogatives as heads of families and to express apprehension that the wife's working and earning might undermine the
husband's self-respect. We recalled this early glimpse of the
prevalence of a covert power struggle in marriage when the
Women Liberation Movement erupted years later. No similar
indications of the "battle of sexes" were found in the Russians'
discussions of the same episode. We have heard the opinion expressed that Russian women are not a threat to men because

they are more subjugated than are their American sisters and more acceptant of their inferior status. Formulated in this general way, the hypothesis is as difficult to prove as it is to disprove. Perhaps Russian peasants and workers are not as far removed as Americans from a matter-of-course acceptance of the patriarchal family; the women of the intelligentsia, however, fought their emancipation battles quite early and have had much more success than their American counterparts in infiltrating certain professions, such as medicine.

Whatever the reasons, our Russian subjects usually discussed the problem faced by the couple of Episode 9 in terms of realities affecting the family as a whole: which job brings in more money, which location offers better living conditions, does the distance between the two cities permit frequent visiting? Some expressed, without much emphasis, the traditional view of the husband's primacy, but no one made mention of any threats to either his or the wife's self-respect. The risk the woman would be taking by spending long periods of time away from her husband is simply that he might "find himself another".

The different degree of conflict between individuality and group-belongingness felt by the two national groups might be explained either by difference of basic ideology or by difference of actual social relatedness, or by a combination of both factors. While the old and persisting Russian tradition places great emphasis on group or community, American ideology stresses the rights of the individual; one might argue that for the Americans these two basic values are more nearly equal in weight and consequently produce a greater conflict. Some of the test data support this interpretation. On the other hand, the fact that the American subjects perceived the individual as being more isolated and more afraid of isolation suggest that they find it more difficult than the Russians to achieve the wished-for belongingness with others. They may, therefore, feel that these tenuous ties are endangered by the ideologically demanded self-assertion, and that a person may be tempted to yield this ideal in fact, if not in profession of faith. Riesman has focused his description of the American social scene on some consequences of this situation. The Russians' greater security in relation to others saves them from having to face the difficult choice be-

Important

tween two undesirable states—yielding one's integrity or feeling isolated and lonely; consequently, this whole area is less conflict-laden for them than for the comparison group.

In summary, an analysis of the projective test responses led to the following inferences about the characteristics of the Russian subjects' cognition and evaluation of persons. Their social perception is marked by richness, is relatively non-stereotyped, and is suffused with evaluations. The evaluation of the other is less strongly determined by assumptions about his liking or disliking the perceiver than is the case with the American subjects, who are much more concerned about public opinion. In perceiving and evaluating a person, the Russians are oriented toward his motives and feelings, and pay less attention than do the Americans to his performance, surface behavior, and physical appearance; while the Americans stress capacity for achievement in their evaluations of people, the Russians stress ethical standards of interpersonal behavior. As a correlate of their orientation toward the deeper personal levels, the Russian subjects display an implicit awareness of the fact that another's real attitudes and intentions are not immediately obvious to the observer; this awareness, combined with fearful anticipations generated or enhanced by their life experiences, creates a strong focus on the issue of who can and who cannot be trusted. By comparison with the American subjects, who tend to emphasize the positive, the Russians freely perceive both positive and negative properties in people, even in those to whom they are close. However, this perception does not lead to any greater severity in their judgment of people. In particular, the Russians—perhaps because they place less value on activity, control, and independence—are more accepting than the Americans of impulsive behavior or indulgence in sensual pleasures, and of passive wishes and attitudes.

In their perception of the causes of people's feelings and actions, the Russian subjects take into consideration the forces that impinge upon them from outside, from the total environment. Their expectations of this environment are much more negative than are those of the Americans and also more than their own expectations with regard to particular people. This realization of the strength of the environmental pressures in

determining people's actions may be a factor in their relative
tolerance of human imperfections, even when they represent
violations of the values they cherish. In contrast to their negative perception of the wider social environment, their immediate human environment seems to harbor few threats for the
Russian subjects. They perceive the person not as an isolated
entity, but as dynamically and actively interrelated with others:
this state of interdependence is accepted by them in a very
positive fashion, without the great misgivings about the possible danger to personal integrity which are manifested by the
Americans. The Russians also show less fear and avoidance of
interpersonal conflict, and their perception and evaluation of
a given person is not influenced very strongly by a temporary
state of disagreement.

All these characteristics of the Russians' social perception
may be viewed as indicating a relative adequacy and maturity of
this function. A developed perception of physical objects is
marked by an adequate differentiation of their parts and a clear
delimitation from the background. Such differentiation is necessary if the perceiver is to attribute correctly some aspects of the
perceived configuration to the object itself, others to its position in the field—for example, its distance from the observer,
from other objects, or from sources of illumination. With the
field conditions thus taken into account, the resulting perception of objects is marked by stability, by the so-called perceptual
constancies: constancy of size, shape, color. Analogously, perception of human events, that is both richly differentiated and
hierarchically organized, that focuses on the person's motivational core and yet takes into account the environmental forces
impinging upon him, is likely to result in stable and adequate
percepts of persons, and may well be considered to represent a
high level of development.

The categories used in the present study, if studied and measured systematically in simplified experimental setups, might
provide common denominators of social perception and the perceiver's personality traits and help to explain many of the em-
pirical findings in the area of perception and personality.

With regard to the more specific goal of this study—that of
contributing to the description of the modal personality of the

Russians—there remains the task of pointing out the limitations that the data and the approach impose on generalizations. I shall not attempt to answer the question of the genesis of the patterns described, as even a tentative and speculative answer would require consideration of a wide range of historical and cultural factors transcending the confines of this study.

The methodological limitations of the study need not be dwelt upon. The two small national samples studied cannot be considered representative of the total national populations, and, in spite of rather careful matching for selected variables, they are in many important respects not comparable. They are not and could not have been equated for the subjects' life situations, present and past, or for the nature of their motivation for participation in the study. The American comparison group is not, strictly speaking, a control group for the Russians, and the differences brought out by these comparisons must be regarded as being merely suggestive of the possible differences between the two national populations. On the other hand, the findings show a high degree of congruence with many of the psychological descriptions and self-descriptions of the Russians that are based on observations and on studies of Russian cultural products, most of which antedate the Soviet period.

It is perhaps more important to point out the less obvious qualifications which are inherent in the nature of the categories used: the limitation of the discussion to cognitive and evaluative functions restricts the scope of the conclusions that can be justifiably drawn. Even if social perception may be assumed to be a function, or an aspect, of personality, it cannot be assumed to reflect the total range of its structural and dynamic characteristics. Therefore the statement that the Russians' social perception shows a high level of development cannot be construed to imply an equally high maturity of behavior, or of the total personality, although efficient perception appears to be one important component of psychological health.

One example may serve to demonstrate this lack of complete parallelism. One might expect that the Russian subjects' acute awareness of the individual differences in trustworthiness would serve to protect them against incautious behavior and misplaced trust. Yet, while such adaptive behavior was observed in some,

it did not seem typical of the majority. Along with initial suspiciousness we encountered many instances of drastic deviation
from desirable caution, deviations caused by impulsiveness rather than by lack of insight. It follows that the personological
significance of the findings concerning the Russians' social perception can be adequately evaluated only within a wider context
of the description of the total personality, a description which
must be based on detailed analyses of a wide range of single cases.

Some additional inferences about the Russian group can be
drawn from the differentiation of the sample with regard to the
development of social perception. On the basis of a review of
the tests and interviews, the Russian subjects were divided into
two subgroups: those in whom the distinctive characteristics of
social perception described above were clearly present, and
those in whom they either were absent or were present only in
a minimal degree. The first group comprised about 60 percent
of the sample; of the men whose cases were presented here
Michael, Alexei, Peter, and Vasilii belong to it, Vladimir and
Nikolai do not. The modal pattern was found not to be related
to age, but clearly related to the combined educational-occupa-
tional level. It predominated on the lower and, to a somewhat
lesser extent, on the middle levels, but it was clearly present in
only one of the thirteen subjects who belonged to professions
or held high managerial positions. This one subject was Michael,
a member of the old intelligentsia but of partly peasant origin,
who had grown up under prerevolutionary conditions.

To the extent that the distribution of the modal pattern in
the sample may be representative of the larger population, it is
probably determined by two main factors: the general socio-
psychological changes coincident to industrialization and urban-
ization, and a selective recruiting of the elite by the present
regime. This selection probably takes place not only deliberately, from above, but also by way of the attraction exercised
on some personality types and not on others by membership
in the ruling group. Our findings suggest that those of the Russians who continue in the pattern of well-developed social perception lack the personality prerequisites for becoming effective functionaries of a totalitarian state. These conclusions

are consistent with those of Dicks (19) who postulates sharp personality differences between the Soviet rulers and the ruled, and they are also borne out by the fact that the regime-propagated image of the ideal Soviet man, with its emphasis on discipline and achievement and on sacrifice of interpersonal ties— is in many essential features the exact opposite of the values that emerge as central for the majority of these subjects.

APPENDIX A

Episodes

Instructions: I shall describe to you a few situations which occur frequently in everyday life, which could also happen to you. Tell me how, in your opinion, each episode is likely to end.

1. A child refuses to go to school; he tells his father that he is afraid of the teacher. What will the father do, and why?

2. A man had asked a friend of his to write a letter of recommendation for him. This friend feels, however, that he cannot honestly write a very favorable recommendation for this man. Before he has decided what to do, the man calls on him to find out whether he has sent the letter. What will the friend do and say in this situation, and why?

3. A foreman tells a workman how he wants him to do a certain piece of work. The workman replies that he will do it differently, in his own way, and have it ready in time. The foreman insists that he should do as he is told, but the workman still feels that his method is better. What will the workman do, and why?

4. A father promises to finance his son's studies, but only if the son will study what his father wishes him to. The son, however, has other ideas; he decides to talk the matter over with his father. What will each of them say, and why? What will the outcome be?

5. In a factory where a certain man works all workers are dissatisfied because of an increase in the required rate of production, and they decide to organize a slowdown; but, in order for it to be successful, all workers must take part in it.* This one

---

*To try to organize a slowdown in a Soviet factory was declared by the Russian respondents to be out of the realm of reality. To discuss this episode as presented, they had to locate it in Western Europe (1).

man, however, feels this complaint is not justified, that the required rate is not too high. His friends ask him to join them. What will he do and why?

6. A certain man feels that people are talking about him behind his back. It happened a few times that when he entered the room people stopped talking, or seemed to change the topic of conversation. And now, once again, as he approaches a group of acquaintances, the conversation seems suddenly to stop. What will this man do in this situation, and why?

7. A young man has been living away from his home and many of his ideas have changed. While visiting his family he hears them express some opinions which he no longer shares. What will the young man do, and why?

8. A certain foreman feels that the men working under him are not doing a satisfactory job. He asks his superiors what he should do, and the superior tells him not to worry too much, that things may take care of themselves. But still, day after day, the foreman sees that the output of his shop goes down, while other shops seem to work full speed. What will he do in this situation, and why?

9. In a certain family husband and wife both work. The husband is offered a better job in another city and would love to take it; his wife, however, likes her job and would like to keep it. In discussing the situation, what will each of them say, and why? What will the outcome be?

10. A boy and a girl plan to get married, but the boy is called into the Army; they discuss whether or not they should postpone marriage. What will each of them say, and why? What will the outcome be?

APPENDIX B

*Peter's Beliefs and Description of Social Classes**

Peter's discussions of ideological questions show him to be a very bright, intelligent man who uses his mind in a rather original way. He had a good deal of feeling about the issues discussed, but he tried to reach solutions mainly on the basis of rational consideration of all pertinent points; his emotions did not vitiate his judgment. Implicit in his judgments was a system of moral values which might be described as democratic-Christian-socialist, but he also strongly believed in leadership and its power to guide people for their own good. This belief conflicted somewhat with his democratic attitudes, but it went well with his strong elitist trends. We shall illustrate these points with examples of specific beliefs.

Political Beliefs and Strategies

Peter believed that all industry, both light and heavy, should remain in the hands of the state. All agriculture, however, should be based on individual, not collective, land tenure. The state is to provide social insurance and stimulate small private enterprise. Everyone is to receive at least seven years of free education; the gifted would be entitled to more. Except for agriculture and small enterprise, the economic life of the country and the welfare of its citizens is the responsibility of the state.

Peter believed in a free press, free speech, the self-determination of national minorities, and the legalization of many independent political parties, such as Socialist, Peasant, and even Monarchist. The citizens of his ideal state would enjoy civil liberties and a great deal of personal freedom. The church

*This review of the opinions Peter expressed in the interview on beliefs and values was prepared by Daniel Rosenblatt.

should be independent from the state, both politically and financially, supporting itself not by contributions from the state but by the income from the land it would own.

In envisaging the coming hostilities between the Soviet Union and the West, Peter thought that, if the situation were well handled by us, most of the Soviet population could be enlisted on our side. After the liberation, the rank-and-file membership of the party should not be punished; Peter was quite hopeful that the majority would support the new regime. There were, he felt, not many "ideological" Communists left; he professed a personal liking for the few he had met, as sincere genuine people. Peter was even prepared to allow the high Party officials, the members of the secret police, and the militia to form a separate republic in Siberia. This is an exceptional proposal; these groups were intensely hated, and most respondents wished to see them punished severely. It was one of Peter's dominant sentiments that everyone, no matter who, should be caused as little pain as possible; somehow things should be worked out to everyone's satisfaction.

Peter was not an abstract ideologue, however; he realized that practices based on the social-democratic and Christian sentiments were open to abuses and he wanted to avoid them. He felt, for example, that after the impending war a temporary military dictatorship should be established in the Soviet Union in order to prevent chaos; that the Communist Party should be outlawed immediately after liberation and not too many political parties be allowed at first. He hoped that in this way the mistakes of the February Revolution could be avoided; not threatened by disunity, the new state would have a chance to gain strength and would not fall victim to any one autocratically-inclined party or group. Peter was obviously drawn to a strong government, but one that would work for the people's good, and not autocratically but in constant communication with the governed. While every citizen must "carry out the government's orders necessary for the life of the state...", the government must "listen to the voice of the people". Though much more articulate than most, Peter, like many Russian respondents who expressed similar sentiments, neglected to discuss how this "listening" could be implemented; the organization of the democratic procedure was not part of his experience, or of his concern.

Minorities and Social Classes

Himself a Great Russian, Peter showed no evidence of strong national prejudice. He described the Germans as stingy and mildly reproached the Americans for materialism, whereas "the Russians are governed by an idea, even if it is a bad idea". He saw only minor differences between nationalities in Russia. As a military commander, he had found that the Ukrainians wanted to excel more than did the Russians, so he had tried to make them privates first class whenever possible. The Tatars were none too brave, and the Central Asiatics, cowardly. The Jews were better educated, more able, and had a great thirst for knowledge. He seemed prejudiced in their favor although he had intimately known only a few.

Peter described and discussed at length the social classes in the Soviet Union. Following are some excerpts from these discussions, organized under the main headings of (1) the peasants and (2) the intelligentsia, with cross-comparisons of classes included. The interviewer's remarks are given in parentheses.

1. *The Peasants* (often equated by Peter with Russians in general)

   A. *"Solidity"*

   "The peasant . . . is more solid and more sure of himself than the worker. He always sees his land in front of him and he feels he is the master of his land; his environment has an atmosphere of permanence. He knows that without his land he is nothing. He does not think as fast as the worker, but he thinks more thoroughly . . . . The peasant knows that if he spends his money on drink there will be no more . . . . The peasants are more religious than the other classes, also more moral and honest, they take marriage more seriously . . . . They have this sly attitude at first; you ask them something, and they may at first try and guess what answers you want and try to fabricate them, but when they come to trust you, they talk in a forthright way. They are less developed mentally, but they have a great drive for knowledge, and not just because they know they can get farther with education; curiosity, the wish to learn, and respect for culture are the outstanding virtues of the Russian people."

B. *"Dreams"*

"The peasants believed that Stalin was wise and clever and essentially a man of good intentions. They believed that if Stalin knew what was going on at the bottom, he would do something about it; it was only because he didn't know that he did not remedy matters. Of course, the government knows of this belief, promotes and exploits it in its own interests.

"The partisans whom I captured would tell me about all the wonderful things that were going to happen in the Soviet Union after the war. They would tell me that Stalin had abolished army commissars and commanders of regiments, and now you had officers with big epaulets, and the kolkhozes were going to disappear. As a matter of fact, the government did close its eyes to the proliferation of private garden plots during the war; it deliberately fed these dreams about a better future. These prisoners would say, Why don't you come over to our side? Look how much better things are going to be after the war. That is the kind of dreams that the Russian peasants will cling to. Even some who did not really believe in Stalin's good intentions wrote letters to him, thinking who knows, maybe some good will come of it; they sort of half believed."

C. *Impulsivity, Aggression*

"Two people may be getting along perfectly well, then an insulting word will cause one of them to flare up, and they come to blows. The insult doesn't have to be anything at all. Someone will say, Oh, you Vlasovite, or you partisan, and one man will be without a tooth and the other will have a black eye. But they do not nurse grudges, in this they are different from the Germans. Two days later they'll meet and say, let's forget it, and all will be as if nothing had happened. I myself sometimes start burning up inside when someone insults me . . . . I use great effort to control myself." (He clenched his fists as he described the effort. I asked him why he was different.) "That is because I have read and studied, I am more educated, and I make an effort to control myself . . . . The devil alone knows why the Russians are like that, but God knows they *are* like that."

(I asked him how the Russian responds to insult when he is unable to hit back.) "If the chairman of the village soviet bawls out a peasant for something he hasn't done, the peasant will keep silent and look and act guilty. But inside here (pointing to his stomach) he will be furious and hurt. He will listen quietly and say he was sorry, but inwardly he will be raging. When he gets home he'll get drunk, if he can get vodka, and he'll fight with his wife. But if the argument is with the manager of the collective farm, and the manager makes the same unjust accusation, he will answer back. He is not afraid of the manager in the same way as of the head of the village soviet. After all, he is the farm manager's own man. If he gets him very angry, the manager may make things difficult for him but will never report him."

D. Dual Nature

a. Good and Bad

"The peasants are very good and kind, but there is a dark side to their character; when it is unleashed, they can commit cruel deeds. The government knows about both sides of the peasants' character and plays them for its own purposes. Openly the government makes propaganda for friendship among the various nationalities in the Soviet Union, but secretly it instigates hatred among them. Generally speaking, there is no racial hatred, but there are many poor and ignorant people who are envious of others; they can be easily inspired to hate the Jews for instance, just as the Soviets were able to make the poor peasants hate the rich peasants. If there is no strong government right after the war, there may be trouble. Rumors are cir-

culated among the peasants that it is the Jews, or the Poles,
or the Armenians around Stalin who are keeping the truth
from him, and the peasants are inclined to believe this.
That is the dark side of the peasant's character. Under the
Communist regime with its miseries people have become
worse; they will do vicious things more readily than before,
even do them with pleasure. To save himself a man will destroy his closest relative."

b. Dual Beliefs

(I asked, how could the peasants feel that Stalin's reign
was the reign of Satan, and at the same time believe that
he wished them well but simply didn't know about the injustices done in his name? Peter smiled.) "You don't understand the contradictions of the Russian character. Every
Russian has two souls and typically believes two things at
the same time. The way the peasant works this out, if you
press him on the point he will say that Stalin is heading the
reign of Satan, because of all the terrible things that are
done in his name; when God punishes everybody who has
been connected with the reign of Satan, Stalin will suffer
too. The old peasants also say that the reason for this
whole calamity was their own irreligious or sinful conduct;
so they have to suffer whatever is done to them until God
ends the reign of Satan. Then there will be a free new life."

Peter added that all of humanity was responsible for
the injustices and crimes being committed in the Soviet
Union since the other countries did not do their share to
end communism in the early years when they had a chance.

2. The Intelligentsia and Cross-Class Comparisons

Peter defined a member of the intelligentsia as one who
has had three or four years of schooling after finishing high
school. This definition would exclude himself, but on the other
hand he felt that any officer was to a certain extent an *intelligént.*

A. Leadership

"All the classes—employees, peasants and workers—

are guided by the opinions of the intelligentsia . . . I can't
understand why the United States recently refused admission to students, to the *intelligénts*; they are the most convinced anti-communists. If they stay here in Germany and
are caught and liquidated by the Soviets, the Russian emigration will lose its soul, the masses will be rudderless. Besides, the intelligentsia is propaganda force, the propaganda will be of the utmost importance in the next war.
Passive people are always easier to handle and to defeat
than active ones."

B. *Egalitarianism*

"A true member of the intelligentsia does not act sup-
perior and haughty to the white-collar man or the worker;
he acts as their equal—I mean, if he really is an intelligent
man; he doesn't look down his nose at people in the lower
classes. This egalitarian attitude is not present to the same
degree in the middle ranks of white-collar workers, who
tend to imitate the intelligentsia and try to speak its language.

"The white-collar worker is not really a member of the
intelligentsia, but he is somewhat superior to the worker;
so he tends to show off before the worker and act supercilious. Of course it depends on the person. Say, for instance, a bookkeeper, who is in charge of the payroll, is
sitting and writing in the ledger. A worker comes up to
him and asks, why have they deducted such and such an
amount from my paycheck? If the bookkeeper is a nice
man, he will explain. If not, he will act very busy and say,
well, it says so here, you have to pay, and that's that.
Workers, in turn, look down on the peasants, in the same
way as the white-collar workers look down on manual
workers. But the peasant, though he is less well informed,
is in some ways more sensible than the worker. True, the
worker sees things more realistically, but he keeps changing jobs and therefore he is flighty. He may waste his
money, because he feels there is always another paycheck
coming."

C. Understanding

"When their child refuses to go to school, people from different classes react differently. The peasant will simply pull his ear, punish him, and the child will go; the father will think he is just lazy. A worker will do the same, or else he may say: 'Don't talk nonsense, I am working for you, I am paying'; this is already a bit different. An employee—a *semi-intelligént*—takes a different approach. He talks to the child, finds out why the teacher has punished him, tries to find the cause. The *intelligént* does the same, though it depends on his character—he may get indignant about the school's defects. If he sees that the teacher is not up to par, he may transfer the child to another school . . . . I personally feel he should talk to the teacher and try to understand the soul of the child."

D. Realistic and Critical Attitude

"The peasant is more confident than most other groups that his judgment is right. He just knows that the war is going to make everything much better. The worker tends to vacillate more in his hopes for the future. The white-collar worker figures the pros and cons. The real *intelligént* can trust his judgment because he examines things with a clear eye. If he thinks about the war, he knows that it will not happen right away, and that he must know many things before he can decide whether or not it will do him any good. The peasant is positive that the war will bring changes for the better, but for the *intelligént* the whole thing is hypothetical, something to be considered."

REFERENCES

1. Hanfmann, E. and Getzels, J., "Interpersonal Attitudes of Former Soviet Citizens, as Studied by a Semi-Projective Method", *Psychological Monographs,* 1955, 69, No. 4.

2. Hanfmann, E., "Boris, a Displaced Person", in *Clinical Studies of Personality,* eds. A. Burton & R. E. Harris. (New York: Harper, 1955).

3. Beier, H. and Bauer, R. A., "Oleg: A Member of the Soviet 'Golden Youth'", *The Journal of Abnormal and Social Psychology,* 1955, 51.

4. Beier, H. and Hanfmann, E., "Emotional Attitudes of Former Soviet Citizens, as Studied by the Technique of Projective Questions", *The Journal of Abnormal and Social Psychology,* 1956, 53.

5. Hanfmann, E., "Social Perception in Russian Displaced Persons and an American Comparison Group", *Psychiatry,* 1957, 20.

6. Hanfmann, E. and Beier, H., "The Mental Health of a Group of Russian Displaced Persons", *The American Journal of Orthopsychiatry,* 1958, 28.

7. Inkeles, A., Hanfmann, E. and Beier, H., "Modal Personality and Adjustment to the Soviet Socio-Political System", *Human Relations,* 1958, 11.

8. Bauer, R. A., "The Psychology of the Soviet Middle Elite: Two Case Histories", in *Personality in Nature, Society, and Culture,* eds. C. Kluckhohn, H. A. Murray and D. M. Schneider, 2nd ed. (New York: Knopf, 1953).

9. Rosenblatt, D., "Responses of Former Soviet Citizens to Selected TAT Cards", *The Journal of General Psychology,* 1960, 62.

218   *Six Russian Men — Lives in Turmoil*

10. Angyal, A., *Neurosis and Treatment: A Holistic Theory,* eds. E. Hanfmann and R. M. Jones. (New York: Viking Press, 1973), originally published in 1965.

11. Hanfmann, E., "Application of Holistic Principles to Psychopathology", paper read at the Symposium on Cognitive Processes and Psychopathology, at the meeting of the American Association for the Advancement of Science, Montreal, December, 1964.

12. Smith, M. B., Bruner, J. S. and White, R. W., *Opinions and Personality.* (New York: Wiley, 1956).

13. Bauer, R. A., *Nine Soviet Portraits.* (New York: Wiley, 1955).

14. Sakharov, A. D., *Progress, Coexistence and Intellectual Freedom.* (New York: Norton, 1968).

15. White, R. W., *Lives in Progress.* (New York: Dryden, 1952).

16. Adorno, T. W., Frenkel-Brunswik, E., Levinson, D. J. and Sanford, R. N., *The Authoritarian Personality.* (New York: Harper, 1950).

17. Treadgold, D. W., *Twentieth Century Russia.* (Chicago: Rand McNally, 1959).

18. Von Rauch, G., *A History of Soviet Russia.* (New York: Praeger, 1957).

19. Dicks, H. V., "Observations on Contemporary Russian Behavior", *Human Relations,* 1952, 5.

20. Bronfenbrenner, Urie, *Two Worlds of Childhood: US and USSR.* (New York: Russell Sage Foundation, 1970).